Fast Tracking Your Prosperity

21 Lessons in Professional & Personal Success

Dr. Daniel Margolin

ISBN: 0986087602
ISBN 13: 978-0-9860876-0-8
Library of Congress Control Number: 2014921765
Effective Publications, Oradell, NJ

Contents

* * *

Acknowledgements

* * *

This book was initially intended for my daughter. I was a little older when she was born, and I wanted to make sure that she had a record of what I believed to be important insights. I have often felt that having this type of information from my own grandparents and great-grandparents could be more valuable than gold. Imagine if each generation carefully made records of their wins, losses, attitudes and viewpoints. Wow! My great wish would be for this to start a tradition in my own family; one in which we could pass our hard-won knowledge down to our progeny.

Originally, this information was a simple list of things to watch out for, and things to do. Only after the prodding of some close friends did this expand into a larger format. One of these friends was Anthony Homer, author of numerous books, including "When Rome Falls". As I tinkered on the edge of putting my thoughts onto paper, business consultant Grant Cardone pushed me over the cliff. Grant's incredible energy allowed me to take my abilities to an even higher level.

As I began my journey into the writing of this book, what struck me the most was the incredible number of people who have had a positive influence on my life. I am grateful for my incredible parents, whose support and caring have made my life what it is today. I thank my wonderful sister and her amazing husband, who never cease to impress me. I strive to be the parents that they are.

There are my amazing nephews, whose awesome smiles have brightened my life more than words can say; my beautiful wife and daughter, who have taught me the true meaning of love; my staff, who have humbled me, and make going to work each day an absolute pleasure; my associate, Dr. Mary Ellen Brucato, who pushes me to be a better doctor, simply so that I may keep up with her impressive medical acumen; and my business partner, Justin Feinberg, who can accomplish more work in less time than anyone I have ever met. This book is also to all those, far too numerous to list, who have found it in their hearts to put up with my relentless pushing and obsessive dreaming. Finally, I thank humanitarian, author and religious founder, L. Ron Hubbard, whose teachings have profoundly affected my understanding of business and life.

I hope that you find this book to be as interesting to read as I found it was to write. It represents a lifetime's journey, and it is an attempt to mark the trail for fellow travelers, so that they may have a smoother and more interesting ride. Thank you all.

Daniel Margolin

"I put a little ball at the end, so it looks like it will bounce back."

Introduction

"I couldn't wait for success, so I went ahead without it."
—*Jonathan Winters*

* * *

We live in a time when wisdom is neither sought out nor valued by the majority. We live in a time when perception outweighs reality. We live in a society that has long past succumbed. It could almost be written in stone that anyone reading this book, believing that knowledge and value were synonymous, would belong to a higher echelon of awareness. In my slightly greater than half of a century upon this earth I have witnessed the spiraling deterioration of our social order. I can only imagine a 19th century man's reaction to the values present in this 21st century. Shocked would be the understatement of the year. He might even believe a separate species had evolved, or, dare I say, devolved.

It seems as if giant pods from "Invasion Of The Body Snatchers" have been planted throughout our neighborhoods, with "zombified" caricatures of people stepping out of them. At first glance they look the same as they did, even thirty years ago. They smile and nod, drive and raise families. They speak of dreams, goals and ambitions, yet mostly applied to their favorite football teams. They seem concerned for your well-being, and they always make sure to caution you if you enter a potentially hazardous zone of activity. Yet, you always walk away from conversations feeling lesser, and feeling not quite as powerful as you did when the conversation began. You have been admonished a thousand times for being a dreamer, but thankfully, you have been brought back in line.

God knows what might happen if they actually flowed power in the direction of your dreams. God knows how your life might have blossomed if you had actually written that book you'd only dreamed of, or if you had climbed that mountain you pictured in your mind's eye, or married that man or woman they had been so eager to throw aside.

While it's true that you have at times questioned their foresight, and, deep down, possibly even their motives, it has only been on the rare occasion that you have confronted the culprits face to face. And oh, how foolish they have made you feel when you've dared to doubt their advice, their generosity or their concern. They ask, "How dare you?" Once again you have walked away from the conversation feeling smaller, weaker and less sure of yourself.

And so, you point your head down and shuffle back to your place in line, this time all the more inclined to maintain your eyes downward. You feel slightly less energetic. Like any good little boy or girl, you search for those who are winning, so that you may emulate them. You look to those who have beaten you so that they may become your role model for success, because, after all, they make you feel less powerful, and so by proxy, they must be more powerful. Consciously, or subconsciously, we begin to duplicate their actions and their reactions. We become that which we have opposed. We change from the wild-eyed poet to the harping critic. And why wouldn't we? Obviously, they have this thing called life down pat. They are so forceful and self-assured, and they can never be wrong.

This book, however, is devoted to proving them wrong. and proving you right. Think of it as a wake-up call to those who have been beaten, and still, albeit cautiously, enter the arena; to those who raise their gloves, no longer capable of throwing the knockout punch, yet still capable of a slight bob and a faint weave.

This book is a montage film of fights long past and of swings your opponents have thrown, and how they have reacted in the majority of situations. The same way a fighter studies his opponents' previous battles, you can review this book. It can be a secret weapon to you, your business and your life. It is sacred advice given to you, in your corner, that will end your opponent's reign right now, and before he or she has realized that the odds have dramatically switched in your favor. Ding, ding, ding! Go back to your corner!

While much of this book is based on my opinion, these opinions rest on the life experiences of over 26 years running a medical practice and over 15 years of consulting small business owners. It is not meant to include every technical detail regarding running a successful business. It is, however, designed to enable a mindset that, if adopted, opens the door to a universe of successful actions. There is no reason for a person to accept the limitations placed on them by any other individual.

You see, limitations are solely based on viewpoint. If you believe with all your heart that something will happen, I assure you that it will happen. The only reason it would not happen is if you countered your belief with an opposing one. For instance: "I am going to be successful" could be countered with "I'm really not outgoing enough to be successful," or, "I wish I was more outgoing, so I could be successful," etc.

Books have been written on this phenomenon, and while personal experiences are too numerous to list, I have confirmed this to be true. It is a belief and a faith that something greater than this moment awaits you. Of course, if I thought this concept would be easily accepted, and, even more importantly, widely utilized, this book would end here. Quite frankly, I would like nothing more than to write these two words: the end.

But this is a book of empowerment, and by its title it would imply that the reader, at their starting point of this journey, could benefit from increased power. By defining the ideal viewpoint, we can more readily evaluate where we are in relation to it. By understanding where we are, we can outline what we need to do, say, avoid and participate in, in order to achieve our goal. My personal journey to a higher level of empowerment has had me running head first into more than just a few obstacles. It's had me laid out by more than just a few punches, and yet, ultimately, I'd find myself throwing punches like the pros.

As I, for one, do not like being taken out of the game, laying curled up like a ball in the corner, I have done the one thing that often separates me from those of equal or greater capability. I write everything down. I study my opponent and I look for similarities, patterns and similar approaches. I write down my successful bobs and weaves. I write down my unsuccessful bobs and weaves. I try to make my mistakes once, sometimes twice, but never thrice. Though, even at times, that has not worked out. I hold myself and my journey up, not as an end point, but as a pit-stop, and a destination from which to jump off into even higher levels of ability.

It must be pointed out to you that the voices in your head that question your ability and oppose your personal goals are not your own. They belong to another, or others. Sometimes, this is accidental. More often, though, it is the voice of those who have purposefully and carefully seen to it that you do not reach your full potential.

I envision a world in which dreams can be brought into reality. They envision one in which those around them succeeding would have them easily defeated. Their dreams counter-intuitively include a world of slaves, who are easily manipulated, kept in a cage and brought out only for their own twisted pleasures. Which dream do you embrace? If your answer is the latter, then read no further; you will only be disheartened by the effect a few words can have on the freeing of those around you. If your choice is the former, then read on, my friend. The excitement of a game awaits.

The Future

"Current events form future trends"
— *Gerald Celente,*
Director & Founder Trends Research Institute

* * *

It is often thought that we must turn to carefully-anointed authorities to understand the trends present in our surroundings. We assume that higher-level beings have figured it all out, while we are simply going through our routines on their stage. It may not have occurred to some that the observed obstacles affecting our daily activities can be extrapolated to the larger picture. For example, much of what I point out as personal challenges in this book can be also be seen as challenges in larger socioeconomic spheres. You don't need an expert to tell you what you see. In your own personal microcosm, you can find the larger macrocosm.

My practice affords me the opportunity to interact with hundreds of patients per week, and so several years ago I did a small survey. I interviewed over three hundred patients and asked them whether or not they had recently lost their jobs, were going to lose their jobs or had a marital partner who was in the throes of employment difficulties. The results were shocking: close to 22% of these individuals were either unemployed or would be shortly. This information was in stark contrast to the statistics being touted by the mainstream news organizations, who report these numbers to be closer to 9%. Who do I believe: those shouting at me from inside a well-lit box, or my own lying eyes?

Interestingly, it does take courage to observe what you see. Once you master this ability, however, you can then formulate a strategy to attack, predict and plan the future.

From these and other personal observations, I have concluded that the mainstream media has it all wrong. Our country is in far worse shape than they are leading the citizens to believe. We are on a collision course with a collapsing and devalued paper dollar.

This collapse will make the great depression seem like a kids' ride. The fact that each month our government gives the okay for the privately-owned Federal Reserve to print $89 billion and distribute this money to foreign governments in a scam called "QE3 unlimited" is proof enough[2]. It would be impossible for any government to print this much paper without it massively devaluing the paper owned by its citizens, and it defies logic to consider this anything but ill-fated.

This book is my way of taking responsibility for my observations. It is an alarm I am sounding with only moments to spare. One can only succeed in a game if one can correctly estimate the size of one's opponent. Estimate its capabilities incorrectly, even by a small amount, and all is lost. Correctly estimate, and an appropriate strategy can be amassed.

What we are up against is one hell of a difficult road, but now that you are becoming aware of your opponent's size, I can tell you a small secret. You are much larger and far more capable, and you can win. You can have everything your heart has ever desired, but not by playing at the same pace and with the same rule book. Where you thought you could casually stroll, you will need to sprint. When you thought you could rest comfortably in your hammock, you must jump to your feet. When you thought

2 Fed Announces Unlimited QE3, http://www.usnews.com/news/articles/2012/09/13/fed-announces-unlimited-qe3

you could search once more for the remote, you must burn the midnight oil. We are facing the potential of two futures: one most closely defined by George Orwell in *1984*, or one defined by the limitlessness of your creativity. I can only point out which I would consider the obvious road to travel, however the choice lies deep within you.

In the previous chapters, I spoke of running head first into life's obstacles. The rest of this book will outline 16 of these obstacles. I will describe the obstacle, my personal experience with it and the solution I have found to be most effective in handling the obstacle. Toward the later chapters, I will outline some more offensive strategies.

The Chapter Headings Are As Follows:

2. Don't Mistake Anger for Knowledge
3. Speak up, I Can't Hear You
4. Dancing with Bullies
5. Does Being Nice Get You Ahead?
6. Weeding out Fair- Weather Friends
7. Others' Opinions
8. The Best Way to Take Your Own Advice
9. Controlling the Playing Field
10. You Must Be Joking
11. The Seventh Year Itch: Is It Boredom or Something Else?
12. Is That a Knife in My Back or Are You Just Happy to See Me?
13. Did Someone Just Suck the Energy out of the Room?
14. The Good the Bad and the Ugly
15. Where Have All the People Gone?
16. Accepting without Questioning
17. Keep Your Eyes on the Prize
18. Survival of the Fittest
19. Confronting the Close

Don't Mistake Anger
For Knowledge

* * *

Here is one of my true downfalls, as it was a hard-learned lesson: People who are angry are liars. People who are always angry are putting up an "anger smokescreen" to hide their lack of knowledge or understanding on whatever subject you happen to be addressing them with.

It is a natural reaction to assume that anger is synonymous with certainty. In a world of uncertainty, however, anyone who appears certain is a magnet. This is the mechanism that has elected countless numbers of angry politicians. Bombarded by news stories of economic failures, the people have been beaten by taxation and deluged by stories of political infidelities and crimes. What is then thrown into the mix is the politician who angrily proclaims that they have the answer, and they assure us that they are straightforward. They yell at any public questioning of their intent, because it deeply outrages their "honest core."

Wow! That is a powerful draw, and, unfortunately, it is universal baloney. L. Ron Hubbard describes the angry person's handling of truth as: "Blatant and destructive lying." Rather than listen to a counter-viewpoint, they aggressively focus on the questions we ask them, with intentions of utter destruction. Rather than address a rational concern or an alternative idea, they ask, "exactly who did you get that idea from?" and target the source. The rest of the conversation will not be about your alternative perspective, but about how the source of that perspective is either a criminal, or is, in some way, in disrepute. You will find yourself spending the rest of the time defending the individual, rather than the idea. Usually, of course, this manner gives us such a shock that it never occurs to the defender of the new idea to turn the question around and ask where the other individual got their idea from, and do the same trick.

Politicians aside, this type of personality can easily stop the creative potential of even an established entrepreneur in their tracks. Tell this person about any new venture you are involved in or would like to undertake, and you're in for some serious sabotage. If you walk away from the conversation only slightly less sure of yourself and your venture, consider yourself lucky.

To give you a personal example of this: I have a distant relative (who shall remain nameless). Every time I talk about anything in an enthusiastic manner, she is sure to inform me that I might end up "poking my eye out." Anything I do that has a positive and measurable effect on my life is not even acknowledged, and anything that I've done poorly, or anything I've done that could potentially slow me down, is blown up as the dominant subject of conversation.

You can imagine my shock when, for her birthday, I decided to surprise her with a $25 gift certificate to Barnes & Noble. I figured that since she had such a strong opinion about almost every subject, she must love to read. She thanked me for the present, and then she pulled me aside to tell me how unnecessary it was, and how it was wasted on her since she never read anything. I was startled. I asked, "How do you get all your information? Where do you learn about all the subjects you're so opinionated about?"

Her astonishing answer: CNN. She got her incredibly powerful viewpoint from mainstream news television. What do you say to that? Isn't that revealing?

Now, whether you like CNN, CBS, ABC, Fox or John Stossel, to use any of these incredibly biased stations as your sole source of information is absurd. It is this stupidity that lingers just below the surface of the angry person.

If you see someone who always appears angry, then run, don't walk, away from them. Certainly don't bounce any ideas off of them, expecting any positive energy to flow your way. Don't believe me? As a fun exercise, find an angry person and start talking to them enthusiastically about some project you are involved in. Then stand back and watch the sparks begin to fly.

Speak up, I Can't Hear You

"Silence fell between them, as tangible as the dark tree shadows that fell across their laps and that now seemed to rest upon them as heavily as though they possessed a measurable weight of their own."
- Madeleine L'Engle, A Wrinkle in Time

* * *

When I was thirteen my family moved from Queens, New York to South Brunswick, New Jersey. As my birthday is in early October, I was pretty much always the youngest kid in my class. The New York City school system had an honors program, where if you showed a certain academic ability, you were allowed to skip the eighth grade. I had taken part in that program, and by the time I had moved to New Jersey, I was approximately two years younger than anyone in my class. Combine that with a short stature, a voice that did not change until my later teens, a face full of pimples and, well, you get the picture.

I remember as a kid wondering how the hell I would get through high school without being tortured by the other kids. A saving grace to me was the movie "Death Wish" starring Charles Bronson. My father took me to see it, and I immediately had an affinity to the main character. I went home and watched every Charles Bronson movie I could find. For those of you who don't know anything about Mr. Bronson, his characters were always quiet, but tough. Nobody screwed with Charlie Boy, and so, to a degree, he became the person I chose to emulate. By keeping quiet, I was able to mask my relatively high voice. In fact, I spoke as little as possible. Looking back at those years, I find it amazing that I had as many friends as I did, but in the end it all worked out.

During this difficult period, one classmate stood out above all the others when it came to looking out for me. To this day, I am still not sure why he was so decent to me. His name was Gene and he was this big, incredibly outgoing African American kid. He was probably the most popular kid in the school, and I really looked up to him as a role model. He could walk into a room and open his mouth, and have all the guys cracking up and all the girls swooning. In those days, he was the epitome of cool. Even beyond that, though, he always went out of his way to make me feel welcome. If he was choosing a team for some sporting event, he would always pick me over those who were much better-suited. I never forgot his kindness.

It is with this backdrop that I fast forward ten years. Our high school reunion was coming up. I was not planning on attending until I heard about what had happened to Gene. Having been in a motorcycle accident the year before, he had burns covering a large portion of his body. I was in shock; ten years had passed, and I had never seen nor spoken to him. I would go to the reunion with the sole purpose of telling Gene how much his friendship and decency had meant to me, and the effect that it had on me. Unaware of what his present condition would be like, I felt that it was my turn to return the favor.

As life would have it, I had just started dating this incredibly attractive woman named Christine. She was one of the prettiest women I had ever seen, and some might have said that she was totally out of my league. I was excited to bring her with me, not only because she was such a nice person, but because, selfishly, I wanted to show off a little. From nerd to stud!

Christine and I dressed up in our best and headed for the reunion. When we got to the hall, the maitre d' pointed to the elevator, so we both got in. As the door began to close, Billy (Gene's sidekick) bolted in. Smiling widely, I exclaimed, "Hi Billy, great to see you! Is Gene here?"

As soon as the words left my mouth, a large, gloved hand reached around the closing elevator doors and pushed its way forward. There stood Gene, as happy as ever, drink in hand, laughing like the world was still his stage. I was taken aback for a second. I didn't actually know what to expect. Was his face completely burned? Was he wheelchair-bound? I knew nothing.

Looking directly at him, I could see scarring on the side of his neck, but other than that, and the gloved hand, he looked almost the same as he did ten years earlier. I was so happy that his condition was so much better than I had imagined that I started to get choked up and my eyes began to slightly tear. I didn't know if I should hug him, shake his hand or just blurt out my reason for coming to the reunion.

My words began to form, and I distinctly remember saying, "It's great to see you Gene," only to be hit in the chest with a sort of aggressive, but friendly, shot from Billy.

I turned my attention toward him as he said, grinning, "Dan, you were always stuck up in high school. I hope you changed a little."

Gene and him started laughing, then turned around as the elevator door opened and walked out. I sincerely had no idea what they were talking about. My silence in high school was due to my lack of confidence. Was it perceived by others to be stuck up? How was that even possible? What planet were these guys on?

I walked around the rest of the night in a sort of fog. Billy had made such a startling comment that it took me days to rationalize it. But, when I finally did, I laughed. Gene, my high school role model, had taught me one final lesson. The quiet Charles Bronson model had helped me survive high school, but my silence had created a blank screen around me. Since I was not defining to people who I was, they were able to project upon that blank screen their own version of who I was. You would have to have been brought up on Mars to actually believe that I was confident enough back then to be stuck up.

The blank screen I had created allowed them to project their own life experiences, their own viewpoints and their own prejudices upon me. What an epiphany I had at that moment. The silent demeanor I had adopted so many years earlier had salvaged me at one time, but had now become a detriment. I was not defining myself in anything I was doing. Even in my practice, I was, from a marketing standpoint, just too damn quiet. I was letting the environment define who I was, rather than define who I was myself.

Never again would I be silent, and never again would I allow someone else's viewpoint define me. I would define me. I would write on my own screen, "Like me, hate me or love me—I don't care. For sure, you are going to know who I am, what my thoughts are and what my actual opinions are, not what you think they should be."

The moment I came to that realization, I felt free. I was not Dan emulating Charles Bronson. My opinion would be my opinion, and I would express it as loudly and as often as I could. At the end of the day, you may agree or disagree, but at least you know who stands before you.

When I look around I see so many people, and so many business and practice owners, being defined by someone or something else. This may, in part, be due to our educational system. Children are taught to be seen and not heard. My daughter, in kindergarten, was told by her teachers to keep all conversations to the level of a whisper. Now, how the hell does that prepare a kid for life? It makes you wonder what, exactly, they are being prepared for. Sit down, shut up, move when the bell rings, etc. It seems more like training a prisoner than training someone to be an effective individual.

Yet effective, rugged individualism is the only quality that ever birthed anything worthwhile. It is a jungle out there, and the lions who roar the loudest have the greatest chance for survival. Speak up, because your thoughts are important and your voice needs to be heard.

Dancing with Bullies

"Courage is fire and bullying is smoke."
- Benjamin Disraeli, British conservative statesman and literary figure

* * *

There is nothing I despise quite as much as bullies. For me, though, it's always been a natural reaction to turn toward them, rather than back away from them. I guess, to some degree, this has been a saving grace, as, given my shorter stature and relatively quiet demeanor, you would think that I would have had a lot of stories about them. Actually, there are only two who truly stand out for me as pivotal points in the journey of finding my own self-confidence.

The first incident occurred in the second grade. I was attending Public School # 165, and at the beginning of the day the children would all line up outside. After a head count, they would be marched into their appropriate classrooms. One of the teachers made an announcement that no one was to be chewing gum. As I stood on line, I saw the dominant male of the class, Lloyd, chewing away. For the life of me, I don't know why I did this, but I raised my hand and ratted him out.

The teacher came over and lambasted Lloyd, then thanked me and walked away. Lloyd and his group of buddies went ballistic, and for the rest of the day they taunted me. Unfortunately, they were right. It really wasn't my business, and I felt bad about what I had done immediately. I apologized to Lloyd, but he wanted none of it. As we were leaving class at the end of the day, Mr. Tough Guy himself and three of his friends surrounded me.

"You are dead tomorrow. All four of us are going to beat you up at lunch time. Enjoy your last night at home."

I almost peed in my pants. I didn't know how to react, or what to say or do. I quietly went home, acting completely normal, until right before bedtime. As soon as I hit the bed, the tears started flowing. My dad came over and tried to console me, but I was really freaking out. There were four of them, and one of me. My dad listened to my story, yelled at me for not minding my own business, and then came up with a plan.

He took the large rubber band that we used in those days to hold our books together, tightened it around several of the hardcover books and showed me how to swing it over my head to take out my opponents. I looked at him in disbelief. "You want me to what?"

He wanted me to let them form a circle around me, and then I would start swinging the large books over my head and into at least two of them. The odds would then be a little more in my favor. Now, this was not exactly the way I had envisioned this going. I was thinking of a plan more along the lines of my dad and mom called Lloyd's parents and begging for their son's life. But that was not to be. To put the icing on the cake, while my dad put me to bed, he kissed my forehead and told me that I could not come home unless I beat those kids up. Talk about going from the frying pan into the fire.

The next day I obligingly went to school, and all morning I absorbed the ramifications of yesterday's indiscretion. When the lunch bell rang, I began the long walk down the concrete stairs that led to my potential demise. Reaching the bottom step, I tightened my grip around the rubber band that held my books. I remembered the basic concept my father had taught me: I would wait until they surrounded me before I started swinging. Lloyd and his mini-gang quickly approached me. Lloyd pushed his finger into my chest.

"You're lucky, kid. We're going to let you go this time. But don't you ever mess with me again."

His friends simply turned and started walking away. As Lloyd began to turn and join them, it struck me: I could not go home unless I beat this kid up.

Meekly, I said, "Lloyd, I'm sorry, but my dad won't let me go home unless I beat you up. I have to fight you."

I looked into his eyes, and for the first time I sensed his fear. He was taken off-guard, and as I moved in closer to him I could sense that I had gained the upper hand.

I dropped the books, made a fist and felt a giant rush of self-confidence fill my lungs. This guy was going down, and I was going home. As if in slow motion, I pulled my arm back to release my first blow. At that exact moment, my father emerged from behind a tree. He grabbed me up in his arms, flashed some cockamamie silver badge and shouted that he was the police. Whisking me off in his car, I thought, "Holy Mackerel, what the heck was that?"

First, I could not believe that my father had taken the day off from work to make sure I was not pummeled. It was a touching gesture. Secondly, I was pissed, knowing that I had just gone from tough guy to a laughing stock in the flash of a badge. It was really embarrassing, and when I got back from lunch I was brutalized by the class. They all teased me about my dad pretending to be a police officer, and it took me months to live that down.

Looking back on that experience, I realize that it was my first lesson in standing up for myself. Even though I was the laughing stock of the class, Lloyd never participated in that humor, and our relationship had been changed in a split second. He might have been the dominant male in the class, but from that point on he stayed away from me. That early experience has served me well, not only in building my personal self-confidence, but also in raising my daughter.

Several months ago my daughter started kindergarten. Once a week I try to have a "daughter and daddy day." It's a time when my daughter and I go out for breakfast, go to Chuck E. Cheese's or see a movie, and just hang out. Several weeks into her kindergarten year, we went out for breakfast. She seemed upset, so I asked her if everything was alright. She told me that a girl in her class was making fun of her.

It seems that my daughter was afraid of the monkey bars, and every day at recess another little girl would point it out by yelling to the class that Alexis is afraid of the monkey bars. Then they would tease her. She was deeply upset about this situation. I thought to myself, "Wow, this reversed the flow." Now I was the dad, having to make the difficult call. I thought about my own upbringing, and decided to follow my father's lead.

I told her that the next time this little girl started teasing her, she was to walk over to her and say, "I might be scared of the monkey bars," (getting closer to her), "but I'm not scared of you."

We had this conversation on a Sunday, so all day at work on Monday I waited for a call from the school, wanting to know what kind of maniac would give that type of advice to a kid. But the call never came. I went home that evening, and still no mention of any incident. It was only as I tucked my daughter into bed that she casually stated that she did what I had said. I almost fell over.

Tenuously I asked what had transpired. She said that the girl started teasing her, so she walked over and said, "I might be scared of the monkey bars," (getting a little closer to her), "but I'm not scared of you."

Almost in a state of paralysis, I mumbled, "What happened next?"

My daughter shrugged her shoulders casually and explained that the kid wanted to know if they could be best friends, and now they were. All these years later, I can say thanks to my mom and dad. I never forgot!

The second incident occurred a little later in my life. I had just moved from New York to South Brunswick, NJ. I was thirteen. I took the school bus to South Brunswick High School, and, right from the start of the year, two bigger kids named Dan and Bob started picking on me. They teased me about everything and anything you could imagine. I smiled through the barrage for the first two days, but by the time I got home I was both devastated and enraged. I really did not know what to do. These kids were much bigger than me, but I knew I could not take at least a year of this type of harassment.

On the next day came the straw that broke the camel's back. Riding home on the bus, the intensity of the bullying began to escalate. As I got off the bus, I could feel my eyes tearing. Bob smacked me in the back of my head, shouting some stupid comment. I'll be honest with you: I didn't even hear it, as I had completely zoned out.

It was at that moment that all of the fear left me. It was at that moment that I entered into a level of anger of which I had never realized I was capable.

I got off of the bus, went into my house and put my book bag down. I walked into the garage, grabbed my bicycle and biked over to Bob's house, which was about four blocks away. At that time, I didn't care how big he was, and I didn't even care if he beat the crap out of me. I was finished. I was cooked, and he was never going to bother me again. I would come back every single day until he was defeated.

I walked up to his door and pounded on it. He answered, and I called him every name in the book. I said he seemed real tough with all his buddies around him, so let's see how tough he was on his own. I think he almost soiled his pants. The last thing he was expecting was me showing up at his door "beyond enraged" and "all in."

Surprisingly, he completely backed down, and even apologized. The next day I handled his sidekick the same way, and I was never bothered again. In fact, we even became friends for a short period.

In later years I would utilize this lesson when dealing with business bullies. About ten years into practice, an orthopedic foot surgeon moved into my area. He was vying for a position at St. Peter's Hospital. I was chairman of the Podiatry Department and relatively successful.

I had performed a surgery on a patient who presented for a six month post-operative visit. When I walked into the room, she seemed a little upset with me. I questioned how her foot was doing, and she said it was fine. She was not having any complaints, and the post-operative X-ray looked great. Yet, still, I sensed a slight edge to her. I asked her if everything was alright, as she seemed a little angry with me, and I wasn't sure why that would be.

She informed me that she had just gotten back from having a hip problem evaluated by this orthopedic surgeon. At some point during the course of her examination, he commented on her foot surgery, and said that I had done it wrong. He went on to say that he would have made the incision more to the inner side of her foot. Then he proceeded to bad-mouth the entire podiatric profession.

I smiled, and then yelled for the medical assistant to get his number and get him on the phone. As the treatment room had a phone, we put the call on speaker for the patient to hear. You could have heard a pin drop when the doctor realized who I was, and why I was calling.

I explained that we had a mutual patient, that she was with me and that she explained that he felt that there existed a better way for me to have done the procedure. I asked him why he felt that I had placed the incision in the wrong place. I have never heard someone backpedal so quickly.

"No, she must have misunderstood what I said. I thought you did a great job. I simply mentioned that another way to do it would be to put the incision more to the side."

I explained to him that that was what she had said, and I was only interested in learning. I asked him what the benefits were of doing it that way.

He said that it was really just a matter of preference, and that there was no great benefit. We got off the phone, and the patient and I had a big laugh. You know, that doctor continued to bad-mouth every other podiatrist in the area, but he always spoke nicely of me. It's funny how bullies come in all shapes, sizes, age groups and professions. Invariably, they are the only points in the universe where there is smoke without fire.

On a school bus, power is often judged by size. In business, knowledge is king. On a school bus, how big you are is based more on the luck of the draw and your genetic background. Now, it is certainly true that you can train in martial arts, lift weights or befriend a bodyguard, but in those younger years you are more apt to be the victim of things outside of your immediate control. Your natural abilities, or lack thereof, will either give you a head start or hold you back.

In business, you can always increase your knowledge, you can always learn more, and you can always strategize better. The level of your commitment completely determines the kindness of your environment. If you are knowledgeable, you are golden. If you lack understanding, you won't last in this world. By being knowledgeable in all aspects of business, you can express your strength and guarantee your longevity.

When someone attacks you on grounds that you are familiar with, they have erred. When someone attacks you on grounds that they are familiar with, you are at risk. When you are attacked in areas you have complete confidence in, your reprisal can be swift and often unexpected. People are used to incompetence and slow responses. Surprise them with a response that is immediate and well-targeted. Only a professional, confident and self-assured, can release such an immediate retaliatory barrage. Sun Tzu in "The Technology of War" explains it best: "Attack the enemy at such times and places he is weak or unprepared, appearing at unexpected times and places, taking him by surprise."

Let me give you a little more reality on this subject. In the late 90's, I had the privilege of running a wound care center at one of the local hospitals. Several times a week I would make my rounds, mostly treating diabetic ulcers. Diabetes is a disease in which high sugar levels often create wounds on the foot and leg which require special attention.

It was on one of these rounds that I encountered a rather antagonistic internist. I had asked one of the floor nurses to prepare the patient for me. The nurse's job was to remove the previous dressing and prepare any instruments that might be needed. By doing this, I had more time to review the patient's chart. On this particular afternoon, the nurse set the patient up and then shouted down the hallway.

"Dr. Margolin, room 356 is ready." As I stood up, a gentleman sitting across from me spoke up.

"Are you Dr. Dan Margolin?"

"Yes," I said, smiling and extending my hand in a friendly manner.

"Oh my God, can you stop sending me all of that information about feet? Every time I open my mailbox I've got another letter from you. Why do you keep sending letters? Is your practice doing that poorly?"

I stopped in my tracks, turned my body to the side slightly and directed my hand toward the phone, rather than toward his hand. I dialed zero and had the operator phone my office. When my staff picked up the phone, I told them that I had a doctor who would like to be taken off of our mailing list. I looked up, half smiling, and asked him for his name, which he told me. I told my staff to make sure that he never receives any communication from our office again, whatsoever. I then hung up the phone and began walking toward my patient's room. He stood up and began to walk after me.

"Wait, wait. Seriously, does sending all those letters help your practice?"

Now he was curious. I guess he expected me to start crying, fall down apologizing or in some way make amends for my lack of judgment. Since I had not reacted as he expected, he must have recognized that what I was doing had a more intelligent design. You could see his mind beginning to race. Possibly, he could learn something for his own practice. Once again I smiled.

"You obviously know who I am," I said. "And I have never heard your name mentioned even once, so you decide. Either way, you're off my list."

I then turned and walked toward room 356. I was still smiling because I was excited. I have a great deal of knowledge in marketing, and my concerns regarding it are twofold: my quality must be high enough, and my quantity must be large enough.

One way to confirm the latter is to see if enough harping criticism gets thrown my way. In marketing, if you're sending out the equivalent of a whisper, you'll get no complaints, but you'll also get no results. If you're screaming in the middle of the proverbial business hallway, the "be quiet"'s coming back at you will be your green light, ensuring a job well done. While it might have caused another to stop all outflow immediately, it only had me more excited to increase the quality and volume of my letters.

Once again, this goes back to knowledge. I understood that my purpose aligned more closely with the original definition of a doctor (an educator) rather than the more contemporary definition (a technician). The more modern concept of a physician is that of one who "does something to you." You come in, I give you a pill. Now, granted, there are some very complex technical actions that often do need to be taken, but first and foremost there is education. If a patient understands their ailment and my thought process in its eradication, they get better much more quickly than if I treat them like a car coming in to have its brakes adjusted.

It is a simple extrapolation of this concept to recognize that if I am an educator, then simply educating patients may not reach the boundaries of my responsibility. Extending my boundaries out a little further will encompass other physicians, and even other organizations. Educational letters sent out every few months helps in the fulfilling of this duty.

Because I so strongly understood my purpose and my role in the game of life, his slight jabs simply inspired me to focus my attention toward greater success. That was clearly not his intention. His intention was to decrease my reach.

Bullies in business can best be handled with a lot of knowledge and a little chutzpah (Yiddish term for nerve). In fact, one could argue that knowledge combined with chutzpah makes for the ultimate defense.

Does Being Nice Get You Ahead?

"Commandership is defined as the management ability to get things done, positiveness, prudence and ethics, courage and discipline."
- *Sun Tzu: The Technology of War by Colin I. Thorne.*

* * *

One of the greatest failings of those who should be successful is their desire to help others. Let me explain, and let me preface this by saying that most successful business people want to develop products or services that, at their core, serve to help those around them. This is a wonderful intention, and along with this desire to help is often a profound sense of empathy. Many people who go into medicine do so with the honest desire to cure, to make life better and free of disease, etc.

Actors and writers often proclaim a desire to create a world in which others can escape into. For a few moments they want to take you out of your everyday problems and into the relief of fantasy. Small business owners often find that their happiest moments are those in which they hear of the successful impact their products or services have had on their clientele. This desire to help, combined with this empathy for others, is both good and bad.

It is good because the direction that it initially points most entrepreneurs in is the correct one, and it is for the correct reasons. It is bad, however, because it allows anyone who would derail those goals an achilles heel. For example: how do you, as a doctor, have this great empathy for your patients, and yet not have the same empathy for your staff when they get sick or run into life's problems? The answer is that you don't. You feel for those around you, you develop products to make the world a better place and you wear your heart on your sleeve. Combine these desires with all of the psycho-babble about the importance of "nice" leadership and "nice" work environments, and you have a recipe for financial disaster.

Have you ever looked up the word "nice" in the dictionary? It derives from the words stupid, ignorant and foolish. Now sit back and chew on that for a moment. The word "nice" itself comes from stupid, ignorant and foolish. Have you ever wondered why when you have been nice to people you have often been taken advantage of? Have you ever wondered why being nice is often associated with being weak? It is inherent in the word itself. In fact, it makes me cringe when someone says that I'm "such a nice guy." I like to consider myself an effective guy, and I'm not really sure what being nice has to do with that. Yet, we are often brought up to be nice little boys and girls.

Too frequently, people assume that just because you appear to be nice, you must be a soft target. They can push you around, take advantage of you, etc. "Don't worry, he won't do anything about it, he's a nice guy."

The saying "nice guys finish last" pretty much sums it up. Now, let me clarify: you should be concerned with the welfare of others and you should do all you can do to help the less fortunate, and you should produce great products. You should be interested in other people and you should be an effective and aggressive leader. You should take care of and support your staff. But nice has nothing to do with it!

Because I try to be caring toward people in general, whether it be patients, employees or clients, every once in a while people mistake this quality for weakness. About a year ago I got a phone call from my office. One of our medical assistants would not be in on Saturday. She was giving no notice and was not finding a replacement. She told the office manager that it was simply not her problem. Now, I knew that this was out of character for this particular employee. She was a hard worker, but her weakness was that she could be easily influenced by others. I called her directly, as this was an unusual situation. I needed more information, and when she picked up the phone, I asked her what was going on. Was there a death in her family? Was she ill? Had she lost her mind?

She explained that she didn't think it was a big deal; she just couldn't make it in on Saturday. I calmly asked her if someone had mentioned to her that it would be alright to violate office policy by not finding a replacement, and thus leaving her teammates hanging. She started crying and told me that her direct senior (who shall remain nameless) told her that she could violate policy, and that it was no big deal, and that she could do what she wanted. Holy mackerel, I went ballistic. I called her senior into the office and fired her on the spot. However, I did not fire the medical assistant. Instead, she was put on probation, but I could tell that she was being set up to take the fall. I think that through my swift and no-nonsense actions, I proved that my position was that of someone who is effective, rather than nice.

This was a test of my leadership. The rest of the staff was looking on to see how far they would be able to push the boundaries. It's no different from raising children. When you are leading a group, you had better lead. You had better set a clear direction for your company and set the rules of the game. You had better insist that once those rules are in place that they be followed. If you can't do that, or if you think that I am being a little harsh, you have either never been a leader of a group, or you are just being nice. If you don't set the rules and insist that they be followed, I assure you that someone in your organization will be setting the rules and insisting that you follow them.

Here is an example: I was introduced to a client several years ago. He had a dental practice, and it was doing poorly. I was called in to see his facility, interview his staff and generally get the picture of why this practice was floundering. Once I had done my initial interview, I sat with him. He had been in practice for almost twenty years and had seen approximately the same number of patients per week from the third year onward. We got to talking about leadership, and when I covered this "nice" concept, he jumped up.

"That's me," he exclaimed. "I always try to be nice to everyone. I have an office manager, and she always comes in late. She is never friendly to the patients, and I know that she is the reason that my practice is failing."

Wow, I wasn't expecting that reaction. Comparing what he was saying to my initial impression of this woman, I would say that he was spot-on. This woman was at least one major reason for his practice's difficulties. When I asked him how long she had been with him, he shocked me by saying that she had been there since he started the practice. When I asked him when it was that he realized that she was less than the ideal staff member, he said it was after the third year. When I asked him why he didn't let go of her then, he told me that he had felt bad for her.

Here was a man who had allowed his empathy to destroy not only his practice, but the experiences of his patients for seventeen years. His being nice to this individual overrode his rationality. His empathy blinded him to his lack of concern for his patients. He had forced them to tolerate poor service and hostility, and all because he could not confront this woman. It was all because he thought of himself as a nice guy. He could not step back and see how many people he had allowed to be hurt, because he would not hurt this woman. She was allowed to run rampant, and she was making and enforcing her rules on his practice. Sadly, this happens all the time. The only thing that stands out about this particular incident is the amount of time he allowed for this to go on. Even for most nice guys, this was extraordinary.

In a similar example, last week I received an email from an old client who I had not spoken to in five years. He sent me a note explaining that five years ago I was correct in telling him that he needed to fire his office manager. I had determined that his manager was one of the major reasons his practice was failing. Now, this was not a brilliant deduction; it was beyond obvious. This practice owner finally let her go, and the practice immediately started to pick up.

I wrote him back to find out what had prompted him to finally let this staff member go, and I asked how many patients per week he was now seeing. His answer once again confirms my point on being nice. He did not fire this lady, but instead the lady had suffered from a stroke, and she had to leave for medical reasons. Apologetically, this doctor wrote to me that the reason he had never fired her was because he felt very bad for her, and knew that she would never get a job somewhere else. This woman had left several months ago, and although the practice had been seeing the same small number of patients per week over the last five years prior to her leaving, these past two months had seen a major jump in numbers. I don't know what else to say, other than that leaders lead, or get led.

As a leader, you have to be able to confront people, and be able to do so for a variety of reasons. These reasons include sabotage, disrespect, failure to follow the rules, etc. You have to send a clear message that these things will not be tolerated. Many times, having to put a head on a pike is that clear message. As a leader, you have to be aware of even the subtle changes in your environment. They can signal that someone is starting to push your boundaries.

When you walk into your office, the general mood should be one of excitement, as if to say, "let's go after the next goal," or, "let's take the next hill." When you walk in the room and you feel a certain thickness, your ears should perk up. When the atmosphere feels more like people have just finished fighting, than that children have just finished laughing, trouble is potentially brewing. You can certainly feel that difference.

In short, staff members' interactions with each other can make or break the atmosphere. A negative atmosphere can certainly affect the experience of your clientele. When staff members feel like they are in a locker room, and that they can interact with each other in a rude and disrespectful way, deterioration is just around the corner. Someone is starting to push the envelope. It's not okay to have an environment in which staff use profanity or maliciously kid each other about their weight, looks, accent or anything else. It indicates a lack of respect for one another and for your leadership skills. When you see this in your business, I guarantee you that your staff have begun to think of you as a nice guy.

Weeding out
Fair-Weather Friends

"Friendship is the hardest thing in the world to explain. It's not something you learn in school. But if you haven't learned the meaning of friendship, you really haven't learned anything."
—*Muhammad Ali*

* * *

There are some people you meet in life who you instantly connect with. For whatever reason, you hit it off. Unfortunately, sometimes you'll find that these people fall into the category of "fair-weather friends." Now, let me clarify what I mean by fair-weather friends: I mean that when you are doing poorly, they are your best friend, and when you are cruising along, they are your less than enthusiastic sidekick.

I will tell you a personal story about this type of individual, but before I do, I have to laugh at a saying that Samuel Markantone, the father of a *true* friend, told me when I was younger: "In life, you will have a few friends and a lot of acquaintances." At the time, I thought he was, at best, misguided. I had tons of friends. What was he talking about? Looking back on that conversation, though, I realize that truer words have never been spoken.

In 1987 I did a podiatric surgical residency at Beth Israel Hospital in Passaic, NJ. On the first day of my residency my father got into a horrible car accident, and we were unsure as to whether or not he would be able to walk. Thank God he recovered, but hindsight is 20/20, and at the time that I was starting a residency, dealing with family issues was quite overwhelming.

On my first day of the program I met one of the director's associates, whose name was Ben. Ben was a big, jovial type of guy, and when he heard my tale of woe, he went out of his way to make sure that the first week's transition was as tolerable as possible.

We really bonded when, during our first surgical case together, the attending doctor walked out just as the case had begun. This attending doctor was supposed to instruct us on how to perform the procedure. Instead, he simply walked out at the beginning of the case, saying that it was a small procedure, and that he was sure we would figure it out. Now, looking back 26 years later, he was right. It was a small hammertoe procedure.

A hammertoe is a curly toe that can rub up against the patient's shoe and become painful. The surgical procedure to correct this requires finding the offending joint and removing the portion of bone that is causing the painful pressure. It's relatively easy to do, once you've done 20 or 30 of them.

The hammertoe happened to be on the pinky toe, and, even for a seasoned professional, sometimes it does take a minute or so to locate the joint and appropriately begin the procedure. When the attending doctor walked out, I looked at Ben and stated, "I guess we are on our own. How many of these have you done?"

I could see the sweat bead on his brow over the surgical mask. I quickly realized that this was his first. A case which would usually have taken 15 to 20 minutes had stretched out to over an hour as we struggled to find our way surgically into the joint. As luck would have it, we accomplished our mission, sutured it closed, walked out of the operating room and promptly fell to the floor. It was one of those moments that can bond a friendship for life. It was the podiatric equivalent of "taking the beach head." I have to give the attending credit; he was right, and I never had a problem finding that fifth toe joint again. There is nothing like necessity to hone your skills. Still, at the end of the day, that was a pretty crappy thing to do, both the patient and to us. Thank God it all turned out okay.

My residency lasted for one year, and it was brutal. I barely slept and lost close to ten pounds, but through it all Ben remained a loyal sounding board. When I finished my residency I pretty quickly started my own practice, and almost as quickly proceeded toward bankruptcy. With over $200,000 owed in both business loans and student loans (some of these at close to 16% interest) and no business background, the recipe for disaster had been stirred. I will always be grateful to Ben for the many phone calls he had with me, telling me that it would all work out.

Now fast forward five years. At the end of my financial rope, I found out about a business management company in Glendale, California. I flew out and spent a week in training, learning about how to run a practice. It could not have happened at a more cliff-hanging time. I was holding on to the practice by my fingernails.

When I came back from my week of training, I began to clean house. I trained my staff, marketed more effectively and found my inner executive. I remember the day I realized that the practice was going to make it. It was probably six weeks after I had returned. I got into the office early and looked at my schedule, to find that it was almost completely filled. I worked the entire day as if I were on cloud nine. I was going to make it; things were going to be alright. Unless you have lived through a prolonged and difficult time, It's hard to understand the absolute excitement you feel when you get to the other side of the situation.

So was the feeling when I made it home to my apartment that night. I don't remember the ride at all; it was just total glee. It was within this context that I received Ben's phone call around 8:30 pm. We spoke about the day for a little over an hour, and then I took a shower and went to bed. Oddly, when I woke up in the morning I was in the foulest mood of my life. I remember thinking, "Last night I was in the best mood of my life, and this morning I'm in the worst mood. What the hell just happened?"

I began looking back over the evening. Did I have a bad dream? No, the only person I spoke to was Ben. I began to break down the conversation in my head. It had started with me enthusiastically thanking Ben for being such a great friend, and for helping me through the rough times. He was correct; it was all going to work out. But then, to my surprise, he began to grill me. How did I know it was all going to work out? What did I learn, to do unnecessary procedures on patients to fill the book? I had spent the rest of the hour trying to convince Ben that I was not compromising my ethics. It was very strange. It was also very subtle. If it had not been for the massive swing in my mood, I might not have as easily realized where my upset was coming from.

I experimented with my conversations with Ben after that. It became incredibly evident that if I spoke to him about how bad things were going in my life, he was my friend. The minute the conversation became too enthusiastic, he would attack. It might have made sense to just end the friendship, but I still felt some loyalty because of all of the things we had been through. Although our friendship was never the same, whenever we did speak, I would simply keep my enthusiasm in check.

It became more and more apparent that Ben's own life was less than perfect. Unfortunately, he died of a heart attack at the age of 42. Though our friendship, for all intents and purposes, had died on that night so many years earlier, the finality of this loss was quite difficult.

In the end, I keep going back to the advice I was given in my early youth. You have a lot of acquaintances, but only a few friends. Hopefully we can learn from all of them. Always keep your guard up around those who are eagerly willing to assist you when you are down, and seem almost too interested in keeping you that way.

Others' Opinions

"The first principle is that you must not fool yourself, and you are the easiest person to fool."
— *Richard P. Feynman, Nobel Prize- winning physicist*

* * *

One lesson that I have learned the hard way is not taking others' opinions over my own. To do so is, to some degree, the greatest cop-out. You know exactly what you want to do or accomplish, and yet you stop or change direction because someone else believes you should. One major reason for this, I believe, is a lack of commitment, or a lack of knowledge, about what you are trying to accomplish and how to accomplish it. By accepting someone else's goals, it affords you an excuse. "Well, I would have succeeded, but I didn't because of Joe." Or, "I meant to do X, but because of this person, I did Y, and it's all their fault."

In fact, some people use this mechanism for justifying every failure in their lives. "I knew how to do it, but I listened to you and did it your way, and it all went terribly wrong. So it's all your fault!"

This is also a hidden way of controlling people, or, might I say, enslaving people. No better way exists when it comes to controlling someone than by making them feel guilty for what they have done to you, and how they have ruined your life. We have all done this to a greater or lesser degree, and, of course, we've all been on both sides of this situation. If this hits too close to home, remember that this is a book about empowerment. Often times, increasing one's abilities means facing up to uncomfortable truths and pushing through them. Looking in the mirror means being able to confront both the good and the bad. Empowerment means turning the future more toward the good.

Growing up, I had always wanted to be a doctor. It came naturally to me. As I have matured, I've come to realize that the original definition of "doctor" (educator) is even more apropos.

This was fortunately, or unfortunately, the same vision my parents had had for me. Like any dutiful middle class family, the entire push of my youth was toward doing well in school. The idea of studying, limiting my social life and working hard was pounded into me. One might even say overly so. However, it all did work out, and I eventually went on to become a podiatrist.

Once I finished my residency and went into my own practice, the real world kicked me in the teeth. It was far more difficult to survive in practice than I had been led to believe. All of my years of hard work certainly did not appear to be paying off. My lack of business acumen had me searching for anyone and everyone to blame. Unfortunately for my parents, they were the closest target. I actually spent over a year barely speaking to them, as I watched my newly-formed practice head toward bankruptcy.

It was around this time that I hired a business consultant. During one of our first conversations, I proceeded to blame the state of my practice and my life's failures on my parents. I had even forgotten that I had always wanted to be a doctor, and I blamed my parents for forcing me into it. I was going on and on about how victimized I had been, when she stopped me in my tracks with one simple question: what did you do to your parents?

I didn't understand. Hadn't she heard what I just said? Didn't she hear me explain how I was pushed and prodded and made to work toward a goal that was now failing?

I guess she did not hear me, because she simply repeated the question: what did you do to your parents? My perplexed look prompted her further.

She explained to me that I sounded more like a spoiled child, then someone looking to move forward and make a brighter future. To her it seemed that I was searching for an excuse for my failures, rather than a solution to them. The truth behind her observation hit me straight between the eyes. I felt like I had just run head first into a brick wall. I was failing, not because of their advice, but because of my lack of knowledge. I was failing, not because of their pushing me, but because I had not taken full responsibility for my own situation. She was correct: what I had done to them was constantly make them out to be wrong. I had even stopped speaking to them.

This could be considered one of those turning points in one's life that prompts everything to change. Nothing was the same after that moment. I had come of age! The very next day I stopped at a florist shop, then drove over to my parents' house and apologized for my actions. Our relationship to this day is awesome, and I could not ask for more incredible parents.

I also committed myself to learning as much as possible about being an executive, and so I began to take real responsibility for the condition my life had fallen into. Now, this is an example of someone's advice and opinions being beneficial to my livelihood. Often this is not the case, and the advice received is so far from one's goals that the effects can be more than just an inconvenience. Look at your own past goals. What did you honestly want to accomplish? What type of life did you want to have?

Now look at what you have accomplished, and look at the life you are leading. If you are on target, well done! If you are not, where are you? Is there someone else's advice or opinion that your life has turned closer toward than your own? Can you remember when you decided to take their advice over your own? Is there something you feel guilty about, or is there something you feel you owe these individuals? Some debt that you feel needs to still be paid?

Now really take a look at this don't just blow it off. If you have to make up any damage or repay any debt, now might be the time. The whole point of what I am saying is not to make you out to be wrong, and them right. Instead, it is to free you of any guilt you may have toward them, and consequently place you back on track toward living the life that you chose, and not the life they chose for you. If these individuals will not allow you to make up the damage, or keep insisting on your guilt, you might consider separating from them, and surrounding yourself with more accepting people— ones who flow power toward you, not suck it from you.

This should also make the point of directing your future actions towards higher ethics, greater decency. Not only because it is the right thing to do, but also because it gives no one the moral high ground, the altitude from which to pull your strings. This point of being ethical, although certainly not the "rage" in our modern society, has been the subject of authors and opinion leaders through the centuries. In fact, thousands of pages have been written on the subject;

"Virtue is more to be feared than vice, because its excesses are not subject to the regulation of conscience."
—Adam Smith

"I have something that I call my Golden Rule. It goes something like this: 'Do unto others twenty-five percent better than you expect them to do unto you.' ... The twenty-five percent is for error."
—Linus Pauling

"Through our scientific and technological genius, we have made of this world a neighborhood and yet we have not had the ethical commitment to make of it a brotherhood. But somehow, and in some way, we have got to do this. We must all learn to live together as brothers or we will all perish together as fools."
—Martin Luther King Jr.

The concept underscored in these writings can be summarized as;
"CLEAN HANDS MAKE A HAPPY LIFE"
—L. Ron Hubbard

At the end of the day, it is imperative that you listen to people, understand their viewpoints and even accept advice from them when they have demonstrated a desire and ability to help you inch ever closer to your dreams. Accepting advice that is misdirected, simply out of guilt or a desire for excuses, or because you don't want to hurt another person's feelings, is the fastest way I know to an average life. An extraordinary life needs fire. It is impossible to get that fire off of someone else's wood.

When people speak of burning out, this is what they are talking about. They are chewing on someone else's dreams until the taste poisons their soul and shuts down their desires. Instead, find your dreams, make sure they really belong to you and go for it. No excuses! No prisoners! Burn the ships behind you!

The Best Way to Take Your Own Advice

"Drive thy business, let not that drive thee."
—*Benjamin Franklin*

* * *

One of the best pieces of advice I received was from the same business consultant I spoke of in the previous chapter. Prior to hiring the consultant, my solution to a failing practice was opening a second failing practice. My reasoning behind it was that two locations would give me access to twice as many patients. It just seemed logical at the time (the fact that it also doubled my overhead aside). Little did I know that, quite frankly, if you don't know how to run one practice, running two does not in any way solve the problem.

Here was a dilemma: do I close one of the practices and concentrate on learning to be a better executive, or do I keep juggling two practices, and hope I can somehow make it work? I really had a hard time deciding what to do. I had invested in both practices financially and emotionally, and closing one would feel like a major loss.

The consultant's advice was to ask myself what I would tell my best friend to do in this situation. I looked at her for a moment, and told her that I wasn't sure. She explained to me that this was a very important decision, and one which could not be made right

41

at that moment. She advised me to get away from the daily grind and make the decision away from anything that would disrupt my attention. Her solution was to take the weekend off, get in the car and pretend to to be my own best friend, giving myself advice.

Several days later, I got in my car and drove from my home in South Brunswick to Cape May and beyond. I booked a hotel room and stayed overnight. I did exactly what she said: I took the viewpoint of being my own best friend, giving myself the straightforward scoop.

Back and forth, back and forth. I took the situation apart from every angle. Actually getting away from everything and everyone associated with this dilemma made my decision-making abilities, and my sense of clarity, much sharper. I clearly recognized that closing one of the practices and putting all of my energy into building just one was the right course. I could always open other practices at a later time, if I so desired.

The correct answer was much more easily seen by stepping out of the situation and looking at it from the viewpoint of someone else. On my drive home that Sunday afternoon, I decided to treat myself to a movie as a celebration. The movie "Dances With Wolves" starring Kevin Costner had just hit the theaters. As it turned out, the movie was about a man who was on a journey in search of himself. It was quite an apropos ending to the weekend.

The ability to look at your situation from an exterior viewpoint is crucial. Often we are so stuck in our problems that we see no way out. You must ask yourself what advice your best friend would give you, if they knew your situation. Since you should be your own best friend to begin with, why not take a ride and ask?

Controlling the Playing Field

"I do not believe in excuses. I believe in hard work as the prime solvent of life's problems."
— *James Cash Penney, founder J.C. Penney Stores*

* * *

Whatever field you are in or are looking at getting into, it will always have players in it who are directly opposed to your goals and desires. If you are a dentist opening up your first office, I assure you that the dentist down the street, who established his practice ten years earlier, is not that happy about your new endeavor. If you are a small, privately-owned apothecary, the larger chain pharmacy opening up next to you does not have your best interests at heart. And so it goes: no matter the field or the endeavor, there will always be those who are opposed to your success.

For many people, this inspires the "me against them" perspective. These people think, "They are my competition, and I will target them for maximum destruction." Often, though, what this mindset does is create a level of antagonism within the environment that is unnecessary. I can give you a personal example which I am not very proud of, but which did happen.

I was the new podiatrist on the block. I opened up approximately a mile and a half from an older podiatrist, who happened to be on the same hospital staff as I. When I scheduled my first hospital-based surgical procedure, the protocol was that it be overseen by one of the older doctors. This was until the hospital felt confident enough in my abilities and skills to give me full surgical privileges. It was up to me to call the more seasoned doctor, to work out and schedule the procedures with them.

When I called this doctor, scheduling book in hand, I was more than a little surprised when he told me that I was his competition, and that he had no intention of ever helping me. Not only did it give me a bad taste in my mouth toward the overall profession, but it both disheartened and angered me. Needless to say, I found an alternative doctor to oversee me, and quickly achieved full privileges, eventually even chairing the department.

At the moment that this individual threw me to the wolves, he also inadvertently created an enemy. From that day forward, putting him out of business became a driving force for me. I proceeded to plan all of my marketing and promotion with the intention of surrounding his practice. In later years, as I became more highly trained in that arena, it took a heavy toll on his practice, and he eventually closed.

Although I'm sure that his lack of business acumen played a larger roll in his downfall, he certainly didn't need me to attack him. Truth be told, he was not really a bad person, and over the years I have felt bad about the viciousness of my prolonged campaign. At the same time, however, he did not have to turn me against him.

Some of my best friends have been my direct competitors. Why wouldn't they be? We have a great deal in common, and most of them are really good-hearted people. Now, don't get me wrong. If we are competing, the gloves are off, and I will do everything I can, ethically, to best you. Truthfully, though, I will also do everything I can to help you. More times than I can count, I have gone over to my competition and have taught them a multitude of practice management techniques.

By raising the level of the playing field, I raise my own necessity level to be better, and at the end of the day, the only real competition you have is yourself. If you are too worried and focused on your competition, you are not dominating your field; you are missing the boat! Don't worry about your competition. You must work from the mindset that you are your only competition, and that you must dominate your environment.

Let me give you a little more reality on this concept. A dental office can be used as a readily observable example. It is interesting that you can have 20 dental practices open within a small radius of space, and all of them reach the same relative size within the same time period. When you add the 21st dental practice into the area, it also reaches the same level in the same time period. How is that possible? Aren't we limited by the number of patients?

From this observable and commonplace scenario, we can conclude that the environment is big enough to accommodate a great number of practices, and that the limiting factor is one's personal ability, not market saturation. The point is not to focus on your competition, and it's not to use them as an excuse for your inabilities. Dominate your field, worry about improving your own abilities and get better and better at what you do. Look in the mirror, because there, staring back at you, is the only competitor you should focus on.

As a side note: While I was writing this chapter, a very clear example of this demonstrated itself. Four years earlier, an orthopedic surgeon stopped by my office to ask me some questions about the area. He was moving in next door to me, and wanted some information about various subjects. I gathered together as much information as I could, and, several days later, I spent about three hours with this doctor and his wife, reviewing the information, and having a very lovely time. I was excited that I had a new best friend. What an asset we could be to each other, I thought. I could refer to him all of my orthopedic cases, and he could refer to me his podiatric cases. This would be a slam dunk!

Unfortunately, once this doctor was given all of the information he needed, he never spoke to me again. I mean never, ever! If I referred to him a patient, he would bad-mouth me, and he never referred anyone to me. The only time he ever spoke to me in the coming years was to yell at me for my patients being too loud in the waiting room.

What was clear was that I was a lowly podiatrist, and he was "king of the hill." For whatever reason, he could not come to grips with the fact that I was far more successful than he was. Rather than work together and flow power to each other, he allowed his jealousy to poison his playing field.

This very morning, as I walked into my office, he was waiting, business card in hand. I, slightly taken aback, asked him how he was. He explained that things had not gone well for him in private practice, and that he was moving down the street to go work for another doctor. He gave me his new card and mentioned that if I had any orthopedic cases, I could send them to the practice he would be working in.

I shook his hand and watched him walk off into the sunset. As they say, another one bites the dust. What a silly -man He could have had it made! Sadly, some people just can't get out of their own way. Don't be one of them. Instead, always be kind to your external environment, and focus on improving your internal abilities.

You Must Be Joking

"The next time you, as an executive, wonder why you are working so hard, look for the Joker in the deck.
"Humor is one thing. Destroyed organizations and human beings are quite something else.
"It is our business to get the show on the road and get the job done."
—L. Ron Hubbard

* * *

I have always been drawn to funny people. Growing up, one of the funniest people I had ever met was my next door neighbor, Sal. We met when I first moved to New Jersey, and even though we went to different high schools, we were best friends. Some of my best teenage memories involve hanging out with him. We always seemed to get into incredibly comical situations, and he always had a way of making them even more hilarious. I remember once, after I had my driver's license for only a few months, I was driving the car with Sal in the passenger seat. I actually had to pull the car off of the road, because I was laughing so hard that I couldn't see. My eyes had teared up to the point that I could no longer drive. I would not trade those memories for anything.

In retrospect, looking back on what we found funny wasn't really that amusing after all. Most of what Sal would kid around about was other people's weaknesses, and as we got older, the humor became more and more aggressive.

I remember once pulling the car up to some people standing on George Street in New Brunswick, New Jersey, and asking them where George Street was. When they informed us that we were on George Street, we asked where the George Street Playhouse was. Since we were directly in front of the playhouse, they were perplexed. This went on and on, and we laughed, pulling silly pranks like that all day long.

Unfortunately, as we got older, the pranks became less and less funny and more and more dangerous, or just downright mean. Once, Sal, my friend Frankie and I were at a night club. We were having a great time joking around and meeting girls—the usual. As normal, Sal was busting chops, and no one was safe.

On this night, he decided to target the biggest guy in the place. He was relentless, and Frankie and I looked at each other. Was he for real? This guy could eat us for breakfast. But Sal, once locked onto a target, would not let up. I don't remember any of the jokes (or, I should say, comments) that Sal heaved upon this giant, but as he stood up, Sal backpedaled. In fact, he backpedaled right behind us. Frankie and I looked at each other, both aware of where this was going, and we wanted none of it. We looked at Sal. "You're on your own!"

It was the first time I saw Sal back down. He had no problem putting us in harm's way, but when his butt was on the line, he was singing a different tune.

Similarly, that Summer, Sal and I were in my parents' small boat out on Barnegat Bay, and Frankie was following close behind us on his newly acquired waverunner. We were way out, when a storm started to move in. The waves started really picking up, and we decided to head home. Sal was at the wheel, and he floored it, leaving Frankie way, way behind on the runner. I told Sal to slow down and wait for Frankie, as we didn't want him stranded out there. He started making fun of me and asking me if I was Frankie's mother. It caught me off-guard, and I didn't want to seem uncool, so I started laughing. "Alright, let's head in," I agreed.

We made it back home, and Frankie, pissed off as all hell, throttled in an hour later. He really was upset, and rightfully so. When he asked why the hell we would leave him out there, Sal chimed in and explained that I had wanted to get home to use the bathroom. Frankie was so mad at me that I don't think he ever really forgave me. I, on the other hand, was starting to understand another side of Sal.

Although several years of multiple incidents of a similar nature followed, the final straw for me regarding Sal came in my late twenties. I had been in California for a week, and when I returned home there was a message from an insurance company on my answering machine. The message said that I should call them regarding the accident I had been involved in several days earlier. Because I was away, I assumed that they had the wrong number, and never returned the call. The next day another message was left, and again I did not respond.

The following Friday I awoke early to the phone ringing. When I picked it up, I heard the same voice from the message machine, requesting more insurance information. I responded by explaining that I thought they had the wrong number, as I was not involved in any accident. In fact, I was not even in New Jersey during the time period in question. What the woman said next floored me.

She proceeded to tell me my name, my date of birth, my social security number and my driver's license number. She was spot on. What was going on? She told me that I had been in an accident involving five other cars, and that a report was filed with my name as the driver of one of those cars, and that the information she was giving me was that which I had filed on the police report. She said that at the time of the accident, I did not have my driver's license on me, but that I provided the license number, and that I promised that I would shortly provide the actual license. When I asked her what I looked like, she described Sal to a T, and when I asked what car I had been driving, it was Sal's car!

I drove to the police station to look at the actual report. What I saw next sent a chill down my spine. The signature on the report was my signature. It was not close to my signature; it was my signature. Sal had obviously practiced it until it he could copy it exactly. If you had asked me at the time to recall Sal's birth date, I would have been hard-pressed to tell you. Yet, here he knew my birth date, social security number and driver's license number, and he had my signature down cold.

When I called Sal, he seemed surprised that I would be so upset. When I told him that I had driven to the police station, he actually apologized. When asked what the apology was for, specifically, he explained that it was for making me have to take the time to go the police station.

Do you get this subtle misdirection? He was not apologizing for fingering me as the driver of the car. Instead, he was apologizing for the inconvenience caused by my having to drive to the station. As it turns out, he didn't have auto insurance, and was hoping to have my insurance pay for the accident. It was all a big joke to him, as he asked me, "What are you so upset about? It's no big deal. Can't you just help me out? I would do it for you."

And so, there ended a friendship. However, I did learn a lesson which I will not readily forget. Humor can be used in quite a destructive fashion. It can camouflage the actual intentions of an individual. It's a great way to control people: everything is a big joke, even as I stick the knife in your back! What's the big deal? Can't you take a joke?

This is a very prevalent personality type. In fact, most of the sitcoms you see on TV encourage you to emulate this type of person, with their main characters and plot lines reminding you that you just have to learn to not be so serious.

As you grow older, life's experiences should show you the difference between having a sense of humor and making fun of someone's misfortunes. Humor is funny, but making fun of someone who is weaker than you makes you a jerk. Being a jerk (while all the rage in today's society) is destructive to your success, your business and, ultimately, your survival. If your business has staff members who are like this, then let me assure you that you will experience a slow, downward spiral into oblivion. In fact, even the cute, "friendly" jabbing about what you're eating, how you chew it, your accent or your being overly-friendly to patients can create a recipe for disaster.

We recently let a woman go in my office. As it turns out, she had made a litany of offensive comments about her co-workers. The final straw, remarkably, was when she had told a slightly overweight co-worker who was sitting on a stool that it "looked like her ass had swallowed the chair." Even more astonishingly, she had said this in front of all the other staff members and myself. Everyone was obligingly laughing, but I had seen this movie play out too many times. Consequently, she was fired on the spot.

The rest of the staff members were reprimanded for allowing this type of environment to be established in the first place. The goal in my podiatry office is to provide an incredibly high-end service. We strive to treat patients like we would treat our own family, and our devotion to that philosophy extends to our slogan, "You've got a foot doctor in the family." So, I asked, why would we not treat each other the same way? Why would we not strive to create a family-like environment?

By creating an environment in which making fun of each other is the norm, we absolutely destroy the ability to create, reach and shoot for the stars. The unfortunate result of this negative environment is that anyone daring to really step outside the norm would stand out and be targeted. The crucial point here is that we are looking for staff members and friends who are willing to step outside the norm. We desire those who are willing to reach for greatness. By reaching for the stars, we often stand on ladders that can easily be kicked out from under us by those who feel threatened and those who are jealous. As leaders, we must protect those around us, so that they may launch us toward the next great idea.

No one that has ever accomplished anything worthwhile while trying to fit in with the established viewpoint. By protecting those who dare to push the envelope, we ensure that there isn't room for boundaries to develop around their success, or yours. In my opinion, as is evident in my writing, success involves being on both the offense and defense.

The Seventh Year Itch: Is It Boredom or Something Else?

"I've got a great ambition to die of exhaustion rather than boredom."
—*Thomas Carlyle, Scottish philosopher*

* * *

What is one of the greatest destructive forces in business, marriage and life? It's not anger, fear or even apathy. It's boredom.

Things are going okay, you start to fall into a routine, and pretty soon, you're bored. Things keep grinding along, and now you're really bored. This is a creeping epidemic. You struggle to build a business, you finally make it to a stable point, and suddenly you stop pushing to go any further. Your bills are paid and your stomach is fed, and so you must have achieved the American dream. Now, this does not just apply to business owners; it applies to executives, office workers, plumbers, etc.

In my medical practice, I cannot count the number of patients I have met with who would tell me for years about how excited they were for retirement. During every single visit, they would moan about how bad they have it now, but how great it will be next year when they retire. However, three or four years after that long-awaited retirement, they despair over the lack of excitement in their lives since having left their previous career.

Sometimes the grass is greener on the other side, and sometimes it's simply the same grass. Now, I am not saying that retirement is not a worthy goal. I'm simply trying to convey that if you feel bored, you shouldn't change everything in your life simply as a remedy for your boredom. Sometimes, boredom really means that you've already won the game, or at least that you have taken it to a new plateau. The time has come to take it up a notch. Create a bigger game right where you stand, and allow it to expand.

By the late 90's, I had paid off all of my student loan debt. I owned a nice four-bedroom home, I had a booming podiatry practice, and I was chairman of the Podiatry Department at St. Peter's Hospital. Several years earlier, I had brought on board a new management consultant who had helped me achieve this status. As I explained, there comes a crucial and unavoidable point in your life when, after doing the same thing day after day, year after year, boredom sets in.

Thankfully, I can now grasp the fact that boredom simply means that you must create some new excitement around your life. Like an alarm clock, boredom informs you that it's time to set new goals and reach for higher plateaus. While I know this information now, at the time in which this anecdote takes place, I thought the only solution to boredom was to drastically change everything in my life.

It just so happened that the consultant was moving to Florida and was interested in selling his company. I was bored of the practice, and at that point had become trained well enough in business management that I felt buying the company would be an exciting adventure. I made the consultant an offer, sold my practice to my associate, sold my home to the first person that walked through the door and off I went. Several months after having made the decision to drastically change my life, I stood in the doorway of my brand new consulting company.

When I sold the practice to my associate, that baby was organized! Each staff member had written job descriptions. New patients' numbers were graphed and reviewed on a weekly basis. To avoid much of the stress that comes with running a practice, stringent systems were put into place. The practice was handed over in pristine condition, and to this day it continues to run well.

Now, I have to give kudos to the consultant. He sincerely helped me understand how to organize my practice. Therefore, you can imagine that I was taken aback when I discovered that the same level of organization I had applied to my medical practice, under his supervision, had not been applied to his own business! It was the old story of the shoemaker having holes in his own shoes.

I was quite embarrassed that I had not done my homework while acquiring the new business. I had made what I thought was a reasonable assumption: that someone who taught me so well also did what he taught. Assumptions are, however, just that, and when you assume, well, you know the rest.

Suffice it to say, I was yearning for an adventure, and I certainly got more than I had bargained for. It was as though I were starting over. Through another round of adversity, I fought my way back up for the next six years. This fight wasn't just about building the consulting company, but also about rebuilding a podiatry practice. You see, a year later, I realized how much I missed being a podiatrist. I had to admit that I missed the interaction with patients, and I missed the entire environment.

And, so, this admission birthed the adventure of starting two businesses, essentially from scratch, at the exact same time. Looking back on that time period, it's hard for me to imagine the effort that it took to make it all come together. Thankfully, the effort paid off, because both ventures did work out just fine. Still, I couldn't shake the fact that it had taken me six years to get to a place where I could comfortably pay my bills again—a place that was so dissatisfying to me just a few years earlier. You can imagine the lesson I learned.

I was bored because my game had grown too small in comparison to my abilities. What I should have done was congratulate myself for increasing my ability to these new and exciting levels. I should have created a new level of the game; one richer and more challenging than the last. Instead, I crashed the entire game, only to replay it later. The invaluable trick is to always launch to the next level, not crash the game and play it all over again.

Despite the stress and hard work, I can say sincerely that I would not have changed one thing about that experience. Nothing makes you stronger than being thrown into a battle. Nothing can compare to building something with your bare hands, and having to figure it out on the fly, ultimately coming out the victor. No one can ever take that feeling away from you, and no price can ever be placed upon it. That being said, I admit that I certainly could have been wiser in my actions. I realize now that I should have increased the practice, brought on more associates and simply run it from a distance. Without a doubt, starting the consulting company with the practice as its model would have saved myself some excitement, not to mention a lot of finance.

The point to all of this is simple: If something is working, paying the bills, putting food on the table and giving you a stable point from which to leap higher, utilize it. Before throwing in the towel, perfect it. Before kicking it to the curb, search deeper and see if it doesn't still hold some hidden treasures. With fresh eyes, look after it, and bring it to even higher levels. It's only after all of this honest analysis that if you still want to put it behind you, you may go ahead. It's important to remember, however, that it's much easier to build upon something that is viable than to leap into something that is untested.

People get bored. Everybody has their problems. Soon, they look at these problems for so long that they become sick of them. They don't want to confront them, come up with a strategy to solve them or even discuss them with anybody. Here is a fascinating perspective: Close your eyes and imagine that you could take all of your problems and put them in a bag, and then put that bag in a room filled with bags containing the problems of other people.

Given the choice of which bag you would pick up, chances are you would choose your own. You know them, and oddly, to some degree, they are comfortable to you.

When it comes to all the problems and challenges you face, throwing them all away is not the best move. Alternatively, you should create greater, goal-oriented challenges that aim to squash the smaller problems. A challenge that you like will enable you to move forward.

While I strive to make the road toward achieving goals a little smoother, believe that my intention is not to rob your trip of all the excitement and thrill that comes with a journey. Excitement is a controlled adventure in which you get to call the shots, and you're in charge. If you want to have a crazy adventure, try throwing all of your life to the wind. I know the excitement will be breathtaking, and, frankly, you'll either make it or you won't. What is essential to grasp is that if you want an assured ascension, and a truly thrilling game, build upon the viability of that which surrounds you. Branch off from there, and then spread out in as many directions as you'd like. Be as big and expansive as quickly as you can.

If you really look at it, it is almost impossible to be bored on this planet. No matter where you find yourself, you can always build a bigger and more exciting game by creating challenges and moving up, without pressing the restart button. Whatever problems you have, solve them by creating bigger and better problems that you would like to have. When you create problems that you want to solve, life becomes exciting. When life creates them for you, you are on the path to an average life. When life dictates your complaints and challenges, you are merely existing on this planet. However, when you are consciously expanding yourself through thought-out, goal-oriented challenges, you are really playing the game.

Use boredom as the trampoline from which you may jump to greater heights. When your goals reach through the roof, how could you ever have time to complain about boredom? Explore and expand in as many directions as you wish, but remember to always start from a stable point. It is wise to take the easy road and build on what has worked previously.

Is That a Knife in My Back or Are You Just Happy to See Me?

"There are more instances of the abridgment of freedoms of the people by gradual and silent encroachments of those in power than by violent and sudden usurpations."
—*James Madison*

* * *

With shows like NCIS and Homeland dominating the entertainment media, the word "sabotage" gives us vivid images of Russian spies, torture chambers, etc. In this context, it is hard to imagine the smaller sabotages that don't emerge from foreign governments, but, rather, from those in your immediate vicinity.

These betrayals come from countless different sources over the course of your life, and somehow they all meet up, giving you the same result: you succumb before you accomplish what you had set out to do. In fact, if you only thought of saboteurs as movie characters or high-level government agents, then you might not be seeing the forest for the trees. There are subtle sabotages taking place all around you, and it's very likely that you've overlooked them while they have been slowly damaging you, like an illness that you have caught but discovered devastatingly too late.

It's painful enough when you fail because of a lack of commitment, initiative or foresight. However, when that is the case, you can at least muscle up to the bar and accept the blame.

When your failure is caused by others, that is a horse of an entirely different color—a Trojan horse, I might add.

Back in the late 90's, medical insurance companies really began putting the screws on the independent physician's practice. HMOs, tighter regulations and the like began causing doctors to spend more time doing paperwork, forcing us to treat the chart, rather than the patient. Doctors who should have been spending time either educating their patients or themselves on newer, more beneficial procedures and older, more nutritional-based treatments were caught up studying bureaucratic compliance issues. Even back then, the impending takeover of the independent physician's practice, by either the insurance companies or, ultimately, government officials, was strikingly and horrifyingly apparent.

The first whiff I caught of this unsettling change was the decreased payments I was receiving. From when I started in 1987, to 1997, the shift in payments was alarming. It was apparent that these changes were not in the best interest of the practitioner or the patient.

For example: A bunion is a bump of bone on the side of the big toe. The surgical correction to this deformity is usually done in a hospital or outpatient setting. When I started in 1987, the reimbursement for the procedure was between $4,000 and $6,000. By 1997, it was roughly between $500 and $1,200, and included a large portion of the post-operative care. Now, one could effectively argue that doctors were being paid far too much for the procedure in 1987, and I would not necessarily disagree. My point is that the reimbursement to the doctor decreased by approximately 70%, and yet the premiums to the patients did not.

In fact, the premiums paid to the insurance companies markedly increased during this time period. Somewhere along the way, the simple math of it did not add up. If the doctors' decreased reimbursements coincided with a decrease in the insurance premiums, I would have been a great supporter of decreasing cost and increasing efficiencies. However, you cannot argue the point that somewhere along the way the money had disappeared. There were lower reimbursements to doctors, and higher premiums for patients.

The fact that this was happening without a peep from the medical associations, and without even a petition to sign, angered me. I decided that rather than sit back and complain, I would do something. I phoned the New Jersey Podiatry Society and told them that I would like to form a group to study the insurance situation. Luckily, they were kind enough to give me access to their membership.

I sent a letter to the members, clearly stating the problem that I had observed and what I perceived to be the solution. Approximately ten people responded, and we held our first meeting at the society's headquarters. Since I had founded the group, I was, by proxy, chairing the group. I believed that my first order of duty was to come up with a common agreement as to the group's goal, and to write that up as a formal declaration.

By having our goal clearly defined, we could then go on to strategically plan the best way to achieve it. I read aloud the purpose that I had sent out in that introductory letter. I assumed that I was following a logical course, and that its acceptance would be a no-brainer. Boy, was I in for a rude awakening! Once again, I understood why they say to never assume, because when you do, well, you know the rest.

One of the doctors immediately protested. Hurt by the fact that I was chairing the group and making its initial decisions, he declared that he wanted the group to decide everything by vote. Additionally, he wanted the entire membership to decide on the reason for its existence. I sat there with my mouth wide open.

It was obvious that the group was formed based on what I had written in that initial letter, and that the purpose I described was the glue of the group. That purpose was the reason that everybody had woken up so early and had traveled so far. To change that bond or open it up for debate seemed like the stupidest idea I had ever heard of.

Yet, this individual's speech continued on, as he proclaimed that the group was not being formed for us, but for the membership, and that the membership should have the right to determine its larger course. He truly took the wind out of my sails. To my enormous discouragement, I was promptly outvoted, and the group was taken over by him.

Shame on me. If I knew then what I know now, I would have shown him the door immediately. The group was being formed along a specific line, and he was either antagonistic or ambiguous when it came to that line. Either way, he was an enemy to the group and the cause that I believed in so much. Truthfully, he should have been thrown out along with any of his sidekicks.

But instead, to avoid offending anybody, I submitted to my dethroning. His idea was to call all one thousand or so of those in the membership and ask them directly about any problems they were having with insurance reimbursements, and what they thought the group's purpose should be. Well, six months and hundreds of phone calls later, the group became a center for complaining. Each person who called had a specific complaint about a specific billing issue on a specific patient. Of course, each person believed that we should focus on solving their specific complaint. They felt that we should become a billing insurance code complaint department.

As any great saboteur would have it, this individual had changed the function of the group, and had utilized its resources with no product to give back. The group received no payoff for all our hard work, and six months later we had accomplished no more than we had on that first day, except for the fact that our once fresh, excited and enthusiastic members were reduced to a band of beat-up and dejected fools. Amazingly, this individual, finally seeing the destructive path he had led us on, held an emergency meeting. His brilliant conclusion after six grueling months was that, as he described, "We needed to figure out what the group was actually trying to accomplish."

I looked around the room, saw all the depressed faces, and realized that I had had enough. Confidently I stood up and told this individual what he deserved to hear: that he was a fool, and that what he had accomplished was wasting our time for six months. Then I walked out.

Whether intentionally or unintentionally, he had stopped that group dead in its tracks. It was also at that time I realized doctors had become like most people: "sheep-ified." To my discouragement, they would never fight back against the insurance companies, therefore allowing their practices to be taken over. Ultimately, the private practitioner would be defeated. It was a sad realization for me, but luckily I am also in the business of surviving. If there had been a clear winning side with a fighting chance, then that is the side I would have joined.

From that day on, I decided to participate with every insurance company. I figured I would ride this wave for as long as I could, or at least until it crashed into the shore line. I would live to fight another day. Unfortunately, as the shoreline creeps ever closer, my perception has been proven to be correct. Surveys of recent medical residents show that upward of 90% have no hope of starting up their own practice.

Sometimes it's hard to perceive that something has been stolen from you, if you never had it in the first place. The payoff of spending all of those years studying is not just financial. It includes the option of running your own practice, and, ultimately, your own life. There's an intangible value to learning the game of overseeing people, and of putting it all on the line. Only a business or practice owner can completely understand what I am talking about, and unfortunately these individuals are going toward the way of the dinosaur. This shift is also detrimental because it diminishes a major resource in the development of future leaders: their training grounds.

A more recent example of sabotage was almost too painfully obvious for me to observe. I had seen this play before and it was like watching a car wreck in slow motion. You see, my wife is originally from the Bronx. Our computers introduced us through a dating service called "Jdate." We married almost one year to the day of our first encounter. I am fortunate to say that she is one of those people who seems to get prettier with each passing year. Once we married, I moved her out of New York and into Bergen County, New Jersey.

Bergen County is perhaps the only area in the United States that still follows blue laws by the book. Blue laws prevent many types of retail stores from being open on Sundays. Outraged, my wife argued that in a free country the government should not be able to restrict trade on what could be one of the busiest days of the week. The extent of the recession's effect on small business owners only fueled her enthusiasm for the subject.

Growing increasingly passionate about the topic, my wife decided to join a group that was working to get rid of these antiquated laws by bringing them up for vote. These laws had not been voted on for many years, and, given the economic situation in the country, it would seem a fair proposition to at least be able to vote on their future.

I remember how proud my beautiful wife looked when she informed me that she was taking action against these laws, and how she had joined a group that was going to get the vote on the ballot. To get it up for vote, she explained, they needed to have 2,500 signatures.

Now, 2,500 signatures is a hell of a lot of signatures, and my first reaction was to make sure she was positive that 2,500 was the number, and that she had it in writing. I expressed to her that I would hate to see her put in all that work, only to find that this was not the correct number. She called the founding members and was assured that the son of one of them was an attorney, and that he had confirmed that to be the magic number.

From that point on, my weekends were a whirlwind. We spent four months going to every local fair and every township event. I watched as my wife and my five year old daughter gathered the signatures. To this day, I still marvel at my wife's fearlessness when it came to walking up to people, starting conversations regarding the blue laws and getting them to sign on the dotted line. I really got to see another side of her, and I was very impressed. The other members of the group were also present and committed, but the point is that four months of our lives were turned upside down to get those signatures.

Once the 2,500 signature mark was hit, my wife contacted the local media, and they dutifully met her and her group at the courthouse steps. Beaming with pride, they officially presented the signatures, and you can only image their surprise when they found out that the number of signatures required to get that particular law up for vote had been increased several years earlier, to 50,000. 2,500 signatures was a huge amount, but 50,000 was impossible. It could never be done!

I guess that was the point of raising it to that level. The blue laws would never again be up for vote. Interestingly, this was so shocking that a local news program, "Chasing New Jersey," picked the story up and ran a three minute exposé. The piece was based on "The Wizard of Oz," with my wife being Dorothy, and the county clerk, who would not allow any review of the law, being the wizard. Two weeks later, they followed with an equally powerful sequel. Media attention was clearly focused on the group and this law. It was incredible! Unfortunately, the attention was not enough to have the county clerk question this clearly insurmountable obstacle. The law would stand, with no vote allowed.

The only real solution would be an all-out signs-a-waving picket at the courthouse. The point is to strike while the iron is hot, and raise the stakes while the media is focused on the outcome. Hell, pickets were at one time as American as apple pie. We quickly learned, however, that any suggestion of protest was met with a startlingly serious kabash by the higher group members. Several of the founding members did not want to be considered too "radical," so they would handle it quietly. They would gather the 50,000 signatures and move on. I couldn't help but laugh. Here, again, was an incarnation of the saboteur. Naturally, there was no chance on earth that you could get volunteers to go door to door to acquire signatures of approximately ten percent of the population of Bergen County. All it would result in would be getting the few people who might be fully committed to the purpose to burn out, and therefore get no real result. They would inevitably slide quietly into obscurity.

The same individual who was in charge of steering the group was adamant about not rocking the boat. He did not want too much publicity. NEWSFLASH: If you are trying to do something, sell something or become something, there is no such thing as too much publicity!

Of course, my wife quit the group. I could say that they wasted our time, but on the flip side I got to spend a lot of one on one time with my daughter. To my joy, I got to see another side of my wife that was genuinely admirable, and, of course, I got a good story out of it. What comes to mind is the old adage in which someone hands you lemons and you make lemonade.

One final note: After my wife resigned, she received an email from the group asking if she would forward a request to me. The group was looking for some more publicity, as it had pretty much dried up. They knew that I owned a consulting company, and that we had a video production facility (my company makes training videos for business and practice owners). They wondered if I could make a video for them that could be used to get renewed publicity. You can probably figure out what my answer was. Nothing upsets me more than someone purposely wasting my time and resources.

Remember this: whether intentionally or unintentionally, the saboteur will always misdirect your purpose and waste the resources of the organization or the individual.

Did Someone Just Suck the Energy out of the Room?

"If everything seems under control, you're just not going fast enough."
—Mario Andretti, Champion Race Car Driver

* * *

There's a timeless observation that indicates that people mimic those with whom they frequently spend time. If you had a child in high school, almost certainly you would prefer that he/she were part of the "intellectual" crowd, as opposed to the "burnout" crowd. You would assume that he/she would have a better chance of staying out of trouble should they spend their time with "A" students. We are all familiar with how the media likes to portray the "burnout" crowd: dark, brooding and cool. Alternatively, the "intellectual" crowd is portrayed as a bunch of nerdy losers. Still, if we were given the choice, those with intellect seem far more sound to us than those who are headed to "Burnoutsville."

Sadly, it is the incessant media pressure to be "cool" that manages to muddy the waters and make us question the qualities that we aspire to. As human beings, naturally, we all have desire to be liked and admired. If society agrees that "dumb is in" then we may feel pulled in that direction.

There are undeniable trends in the media that favor superficiality and a lack of intellect. Natural law, however, favors those who are fit enough to survive. Those who are aware of their present and future obstacles, with their efforts devoted to overcoming these obstacles, are the people who fare better. Intellect, the appropriate education and awareness historically lead to a longer and more prosperous survival. There exists a social dichotomy, in which on one hand we are drawn to social pressures that tell us to be cool, simple-minded and drugged out, while natural law clearly favors the strong.

The choice should be obvious. Yet, growing up, I was surrounded by those whose goals and intellect did not exceed what seemed like a sixth grade level. It actually put me in a tough spot, as I felt drawn to the desire to fit in. It took me more than a few years to have enough faith in myself to begin to separate from the "in crowd", or, should I say, the obsessive desire to be part of that crowd. It didn't happen overnight.

Honestly, I found a strangely comforting appeal in what looked "normal": working 9-5, and then hitting the bars to talk about how crappy the day was. The middle class social norm favors the middle class social norm, even though the norm feels like an octopus wrapping its stifling tentacles around you from all directions.

Living an average lifestyle begets an average life. Alarmingly, though, the quality of the middle class lifestyle is in rapid decline. We all know that a dollar won't buy you what a dollar bought you last year.

Are you working a 9-5 job (if you can find a job) and doing just enough to get by? If you're lucky, you make just enough to pay the mortgage and take that one-week vacation each year. Five years from now, can you maintain this lifestyle, as the economy changes?

Inflation alone makes the answers to my questions frighteningly obvious. At the end of the day you simply have to work harder. Not one person who really made it on their own got there without working hard. It's just not possible. Even if you have an incredible idea for building a better mouse trap, you still either have to build it or sell it to someone who will. Selling an idea means getting in front of huge quantities of potential buyers. That, my friends, is a lot of work.

Unfortunately, falling into society's trap of striving for stupidity makes us hate the concept of work. We hate everything about working: the rules, the effort and the long hours. Instead of finding value in hard work, and working toward that irreplaceable feeling of accomplishment, we strive to be on a beach with a margarita in hand. Guess what? Go sit on a beach with a margarita for three weeks. Unless you are completely brain-dead, it gets boring as hell, really fast.

Sure, having a couple of days off is great, but if that feels like your life's calling, it's evident that the media has crept into your brain. Goals like that are not inherently human. I have never seen a healthy child who wasn't dreaming about growing up to be an astronaut, president or king. From birth, we are naturally drawn to action and motion. Needless to say, sitting around all day and drinking is not going to fulfill your human instincts. People are inherently drawn to adventure, and it takes a hell of a lot of hours of watching television or playing on your X-Box to break down your human instincts. Yet, amazingly, it has been broken. Apathy has come to America. Once adventurous and fearless, America's spirit has been stolen, but it hasn't been stolen from all of us.

The same way you protect your home from potential predators, you can protect your future. As an alarm system can be set up for your front door, you should have an internal alarm system that detects those around you. I believe that the easiest alarm system to set up is the "energy drain" alarm. We all know someone who, after a long conversation with them, makes us feel completely drained. This is when the bells should go off.

The next alarm is called the "stress" alarm, for someone who gives you that feeling of uneasiness in your gut. You can feel the stress swell up when you're about to meet with them, and deep down you know that you sort of wish they would cancel at the last minute. Alarms should be blaring!

Another alarm is called the "feel worse about myself" alarm. Sometimes there is someone in your life who makes you feel worse about yourself after a conversation. Ding, ding!

Alarms are a defensive strategy. They warn us just before we allow these people to control our lives. Similarly, you need an offensive strategy as well. How about seeking out and surrounding yourself with people who raise the bar for you?

Do you know people who point you in the direction of a more ideal you? I'm not just referring to people who can supply you with money. I'm talking about people whose values and priorities inspire you to be better. At the end of the day, raising the bar for yourself raises the bar for everyone. And wouldn't it be a nicer world if the bar was raised a little higher?

The Good the Bad
and the Ugly

"Most men would rather die, than think. Many do."
— *Bertrand Russell, British philosopher*

* * *

My maternal grandparents grew up in Germany. As a Jewish kid growing up in Queens, New York, I heard my share of stories about the Holocaust. Our next door neighbor, Henny, had a tattoo on her arm with the concentration camp numbers clearly marking her past. To this day, I do not understand how people can be so inhumane.

My grandfather lived in Breslau, Germany. On the night of the historical event Kristallnacht, the SS took many of the Jewish men, "for their own good," to the camps. My grandfather was taken to Buchenwald, along with many of his relatives.

My grandfather was a boxer in Germany, and his face bore the scars of his career. As a child, I was in awe of the toughness of his face. He had a crushed nose and a slight case of cauliflower ear.

Shortly after coming to America, he was walking by himself one night. A mugger grabbed him by the shoulder and spun him around. He then took one look at my grandfather's face, and just started running. Needless to say, this was probably a smart idea.

Another story involves him and a friend walking home one night after curfew, in Germany. They were approached by two Gestapo officers who demanded their papers. They had left their papers behind, and instantly recognized the danger of the situation. My grandfather grabbed the back of one of the soldier's helmets and smashed his fist into his face. His friend instantly did the same. They walked away leaving the two SS unconscious on the floor. This was a display of courage that is difficult to imagine. It's almost superhuman. But I digress.

Having grown up in Germany, he had trained many of the Nazis in boxing during their younger years. Some of his captors in Buchenwald had once been his students. On the first night in captivity, one of the soldiers pulled him to the side and told him that the next morning he would be asking for volunteers to clean his office. The soldier explained that my grandfather should volunteer, as he had very important information to share with him. The next morning, he obligingly stepped out of line. His male relatives stood in disbelief, whispering to him in German, "What the hell are you doing?" Once in his office, the soldier locked the door.

"Dago," the solder said, "the plan is that they are going to kill all of you. You have to sell everything and get out of the country. I will get word back to your wife, but you must leave as quickly as possible. There is no time."

Of course, this was rather startling news. The propaganda line had been that the Jewish men were being taken away for their own protection. The Germans were so mad at the Jews that the only way to guarantee their safety was in the camps. The officer kindly gave my grandfather a long black jacket, its pockets filled with chocolate. The length of the jacket allowed him to go to the bathroom without being noticed (prisoners were routinely beaten simply for urinating).

The soldier made Dago promise never to contact his mother to thank her for her son's actions. This Nazi had no illusions, as he knew that his own mother would turn him in, and that he would be put to death. They shook hands and went back to their respective roles.

Many people don't know that when the camps first opened, if you sold all your belongings and bought tickets out of the country, you were allowed to leave. Buchenwald allowed this for only the first two weeks. My grandfather left the day before this escape method was disallowed. When he went back to his relatives to explain what had just transpired, they laughed. No way were the Nazis going to kill them, they thought. They were there for protection. No way would the soldiers, who they had also grown up with, kill them.

One must understand that these people were trapped. They were watching fellow Jews being beaten on an hourly basis. They were being starved, and in just under two weeks my grandfather lost 40 lbs. Still, somehow, these people could not be convinced of their captor's evil intentions.

My grandfather left, and my understanding is that the majority of his family perished. The lesson here for all of us is that you shouldn't justify your surroundings, but rather you should observe them. They are what they are, and not what you would like them to be. Evil exists, and for the sake of its power, it tries to convince you that it does not exist at all.

Even today, I believe that most people, given a good enough propaganda line, would happily stay in those camps without thinking anything of it. I am extremely proud of my grandfather, because it took profound courage to observe what he observed, and to take action when those around him froze. They left Germany, and, to make a long story short, they ended up in Shanghai.

At the time, Shanghai was one of the few cities that would accept the Jewish refugees. I wish I had more information about how they survived there, and what their lives there were like. There, in Shanghai, was the birth place of my mother, and from there they went to Israel, and eventually Queens. This is where my mother, in her teen years at a Jewish singles' dance, fortuitously met my father.

Naturally, growing up I loved to hear stories about my grandfather. Sadly for me, however, he never really spoke much about those days. It was only my incessant curiosity that forced him to shed some light on his fascinating history.

I have found that survivors of these atrocities have adopted two different mindsets: either the survivors exist in a state of continued devastation, or they are grateful for the chance to appreciate the true beauty in their lives. My grandfather's mindset was that of the latter. He was always tremendously optimistic. He was always smiling, yet he was always quiet.

Each week, he and my grandmother would come over to our apartment and take our family out to dinner. This was a ritual that went on for countless years. He would sit at the head of the table, never speaking, yet always smiling. I won't forget how he would look at my sister and me as if we were diamonds he had just found under an old suitcase. As we got older, my sister and I teased him about his silence.

"Dago, why do you never speak when we eat dinner? You just sit and smile at us." His response expressed gratitude for what he had. I could only really understand this response fully in my later years. Quite simply, he was overjoyed to be with his family. The feelings he received from being able to provide for us he could never express in words.

That was my maternal family. However, on my dad's side, the story is slightly different. My paternal grandmother, coming from a home of violence, had escaped Poland as a child. She came from seriously tough people. For instance, my grandmother's brother, Mack, told stories of how, when he first came to America, his father took Mack to work with him. His father (my great-grandfather) was a strong arm for a loan shark. Mack got to watch his old man break someone's leg with a metal pipe. Isn't that a "nice" example of father and son bonding?

His wife Tillie, who was my great-grandmother, also came from incredibly tough stock. She died at the age of 105, and I can clearly remember her dancing wildly at her 100th birthday party. The craziest story about her I ever heard involved a fistfight she got into at the age of 97. She was living in the Jewish home for the aged in the Bronx. One of the attendants was a young Spanish man who loved to kid around with her and her roommate. One day, when he left the room, Tillie and her roommate got into a heated argument over the subject of which woman he liked better. Believe it or not, it almost immediately escalated into full-out fisticuffs, concluding with my great-grandmother knocking out her roommate over the bed.

My paternal grandparents met and raised a family in Astoria, Queens. To be perfectly truthful, my grandmother, Jean, was one of the most difficult people I have ever met. Jean was one of those people who just exuded misery, and because she would wake up in such foul moods, my father tells stories about how he and his brothers would make a run for it, out of the house, each morning.

Somehow, my grandfather, Murray, was the complete opposite. He was a mild, all-around nice guy. He worked as a waiter. In fact, I truly believe that he worked three jobs just to stay as far away from her as possible. When I was twelve, we were stunned at the news that a fire in my grandparents' apartment complex had claimed his life. Needless to say, I was devastated, especially as this marked the first time that I had faced the death of a close relative.

After sitting shiva (mourning) for a week, my father went back to the apartment to retrieve some of my grandmother's items. While my father was rummaging through the apartment, one of the neighbors approached him and kindly expressed his condolences regarding my grandfather's death. The neighbor proceeded to explain that what was especially devastating to him was witnessing my grandfather returning to the burning home after he had safely made it out.

My father was aghast. He did not know that his father had made it out. As far as my father was concerned, my grandfather had gone to bed the evening before, and simply had never awoken. My grandmother claimed that she never even saw him. The neighbor, however, was adamant, as he had been standing next to my grandparents on the sidewalk. To my father's surprise, he continued to explain that he had heard Jean screaming at Murray to go back into the apartment and fetch her pocketbook. Ultimately, he died obeying his wife's commands.

The fact that she had sent him back into the fire was bad enough. The fact that she never told anyone, and expressed no remorse for it, was even worse. But the way that she denied it, even after it was confirmed by a second neighbor, was startling. Now, maybe not everybody would find this as chilling as I do. There are those out there who completely lack a conscience, and perhaps they would do the same exact thing. Please excuse me if you feel that I am being a little too harsh on my poor grandmother. To be fair, she was always pleasant to me. However, I simply observed what I observed.

To give you one final example of her personality type: As the last few weeks of her life were approaching, I decided to visit her in the hospital. My father asked me to spend the day with her to ensure that she was getting the proper medication and adequate nutrition. I sat there with her, and, since we had the whole day ahead of us, I decided to learn a little more about her life.

"Grandma, tell me something about your life." There was a sincere curiosity in my voice.

"What would you like to know?"

"Tell me something good about your life."

She looked perplexed. You could see her eyes squint as she spent 30 seconds in silence, thinking with all her might.

"I can't think of anything."

"So," I reasoned, "tell something bad about your life."

Oh my God, she went off for about two hours. Listening to her tales of misery was so draining that after a certain point, I started going cross-eyed. Finally, I stopped her.

"Okay, okay, I get it!" I exclaimed, desperately. "Now tell me something good about your life," I pleaded.

Once again, she paused. "I can't think of anything."

Prompting her toward the sunlight, I asked, "What about the day you married grandpa?"

Without a beat, she moaned about the excruciating heat on her wedding day. She complained about the difficulties of sweating profusely in a wedding gown.

I started to laugh. We see what we see. I could have had an easier time asking a blind man to drive me home than convince her to see the glass half full.

All these people were the mentors of my youth. Here were the purveyors of my life's lessons. My mother's father had lived through so much, and yet he valued decency above all. My father's mother created a cloud of negativity, and allowed it to shower her wherever she went. There was the Nazi officer, who saved my family. There were those family members who stayed in the camps, because they lacked the foresight and vision to observe their reality.

As it turns out, life is a complex combination of decisions and perspectives. Yet, somehow, through it all, two overriding concepts emanate: good and evil. Both lie just under the surface of the world as it stands today, and as it has stood since time immemorial.

Each of us have our life lessons. Each of us walk away from our youth with viewpoints based on our experiences. Now you have a glimpse into my youth. What perspective would you have taken from my background? How would these stories have influenced you?

As for my perspective, I walked away with a burning desire to survive and to do better. I decided to learn as much as I could, to make the environment safer for my friends and family. I was blessed to not have a false impression of safety. Early on, I realized that many of those people dying in those camps were probably nicer than I was and smarter than I was, and yet the universe did not jump in to save them. If a Nazi soldier was concerned about his own mother turning him in, and if my grandmother could send a man she had been married to for forty years into a fire with no observable remorse, what was this game called life really about? What was I up against? Had it no shame? Had it no boundaries?

Looking around, my friends clearly had no idea about the iron fist under the velvet glove. Life was sports and television. Life in America was freedom, and there were no worries. In a way, this was the typical middle class perspective: work hard, study hard, get a good job, save and raise a family, and, somehow, it will all work out.

Yet I never completely bought in. It always felt like a trap. This lifestyle never seemed to have enough of a safety margin. Something always irritated me and always drove me. Just below the surface, I always felt the need to keep searching, keep learning and never stand still for too long. I decided that I would never be caught standing in line with anyone. I would never voluntarily, or involuntarily, walk into a camp. It took me until my adulthood to realize that this was the correct viewpoint for survival.

"When one thinks of survival, one is apt to make the error of thinking in terms of "barest necessity." That is not survival. For it has no margin for loss."

"In life, the only real guarantee of survival is abundance." -L. Ron Hubbard

For me this means abundance of knowledge, abundance of finance, abundance of friendship, abundance of love, etc.

There was safety in the middle class when I was growing up. It was that kind of comforting safety that my parents strove for. To have your own home and three square meals a day; boy, that was living.

Today, with the excessive printing of money by the government, and regulations either closing businesses or shipping them overseas, the middle class is under attack. This is not the small type of attack that works like a brush fire; it's an all-out war. The middle class is under siege. Today, the idea of striving to be in the middle class by working just hard enough to pay the mortgage is almost futile. The current monetary inflation problem alone should make this obvious. The fact that the government has taken on such extraordinary debt, while much of the public have been conveniently unaware, should be a huge red flag. Only two parties exist, and yet both have taken the country down the same impoverished road. That's some food for thought.

Where Have All
the People Gone?

"As you think, so shall you become."
—Bruce Lee

* * *

Something has changed! People think, act and talk very different than they did several decades ago, and not in a good way. Walk down the street and look at people's faces. They seem distant, lost in their own thoughts, concerned only about their own existence. You are lucky if you can make it through driving somewhere without being cut off or tailgated. People simply aren't paying attention, and you can't just blame it on the fact that everybody is texting while driving. Living on this planet for a few decades gives you an opportunity, if you pay attention: you get to compare today's inhabitants to those of yesteryear. They are different!

The year was 1981, and I was a sophomore at Rutgers University in New Brunswick, New Jersey. My friends Rich, Mike and Mike's girlfriend for a little over a year, Brenda, attended an event on campus. Sandra Bernhard, a comedian, was making the college rounds, and, on this particular night, her opening act was a hypnotist.

At the start of the show, this hypnotist asked for ten volunteers. Mike's girlfriend eagerly jumped up on the stage. Now, hypnotism does not work on everyone, since you have to be susceptible to this type of subconscious manipulation. The very first thing the hypnotist does is determine which of the volunteers would be most vulnerable. Of the ten that night, only two made the cut, and one of them was Brenda.

During the show, the hypnotist had Brenda bark like a dog and quack like a duck, but what really caught my attention was what happened after he asked her for her boyfriend's name. She obligingly told him that it was Mike, and she pointed directly at him. He then told her to close her eyes.

"You will search and search for Mike, but you will not be able to see him. Even if he is standing right in front of you, you will no longer be able to see him." He snapped his fingers, and she ran into the audience to begin her search. She walked up to me, and, in a rather frantic tone, asked me if I had seen Mike. He was standing right next to me. With my mouth wide open, I told her that I had no idea where he was. Disappointed, she declared that she had to find him, and she walked away.

It was an experience that I will always remember. I had witnessed for myself something I would have never otherwise believed. Deep into Brenda's subconscious, the hypnotist had installed a command that overrode her consciousness. For all intents and purposes, she was sleep-walking. Most hypnotists will tell you that the implantation of a command into your subconscious does not have permanent affects, but I am not completely convinced. In fact, Brenda and Mike broke up several weeks later. She made it clear to Mike that she could "no longer see him." I often wonder if that was her, speaking from the heart, or a remnant of that evening.

Flash forward thirty years. My wife, daughter and I were attending the New Jersey State Fair. As we walked through the fairgrounds, an announcement was made that a hypnotist's show was about to start. I asked my wife if she had ever seen a hypnotist, and she told me that she had not. I gave her a quick run-down of the Mike and Brenda story, and off we went to see the show.

This was a much bigger audience than there had been at my previous experience, with well over 200 people in attendance. 20 people went on stage for the preliminary screening. Just as it had happened 30 years earlier, this hypnotist went through some basic steps to evaluate susceptibility, but, this time, the outcome was much different.

Of the 20 who went on stage, only 4 were *not* susceptible. In other words, he found 16 individuals whose minds were vulnerable to his manipulation. The numbers had completely reversed! 30 years ago, only 20% of the participants were potential hypnotic subjects, and today it was 80%. Actually, it was more than 80%, because while the hypnotist was instructing his participants to fall deeper and deeper asleep, a small boy in the front row fell out of his chair and onto the floor, fast asleep. The hypnotist asked the parents if they could bring the boy up on stage, and they agreed. He actually had the boy walk up the stairs to the stage as if he were a chicken. It was startling.

I have never heard anyone else make this connection, but it does explain some of my previous observations. It clarified, for me, that something had transpired with the population over the last few decades. People had gradually become more suggestible, and, therefore, they had been thrown deeper and deeper into sleep. Whether this is the result of chemicals being placed in the water, excessive psychiatric medicating or the return of illicit street drugs is merely speculation. What is factually evident is that something has changed.

A hypnotist performs his feats by having his subject focus their attention fixedly on some random item, like a watch or a spinning wheel. He then uses a command to bypass their very consciousness. The current economic environment also utilizes this technique, by keeping people in such duress that all they can concentrate on is surviving, paying their mortgage and desperately trying not to lose their jobs. Their attention is fixed. Add to this mix a cocktail of drug usage, and it is a miracle that 100% of us are not susceptible to subconscious manipulation.

You ask: So what? The fact that others are asleep has no affect on my life. Well, unfortunately, it affects all of us. It makes the world a more difficult place to live in. Having an intelligent conversation with the majority of people is becoming a feat. Most people do not think; they simply react. You say hello, and they say hello. You say goodbye, and they say goodbye.

Have you ever been drunk? I mean, have you ever been really sloshed? If you're in the majority, the answer is yes. Now imagine that, while intoxicated, you were asked to perform a complex mathematical equation, or perhaps, even, a relatively simple one. Chances are that you would have a somewhat difficult time. The highest level of function you could perform would be to follow a very straightforward and direct command: Sit down! Stand Up! Have another drink!

Now imagine that this was your permanent state. What would the implications of that be, not only for you, but for those around you?

Fifteen years ago I began working with business owners. While it was difficult even then for me to get them to realize how their actions were negatively affecting their businesses, once they were clearly shown the direct results of their lack of business sense, they quickly corrected themselves and maintained their new ways. This happens less and less today.

Today, if you can get business owners to see the err of their ways, you often have to do it again two weeks later. They don't remember, they can't react and they are easily distracted. It is as if they have reverted back to childhood. Instead of working with them as peers, I am finding that the relationships frequently resemble that of a father speaking to his child. My role has become one in which I have to continuously remind them of what they had recognized and agreed to accomplish only weeks earlier.

My company is called Effective Management, and I am the founder and co-owner. We produce several training products.

One is called "Winning Business Tips," and it is a free video series designed to help business and practice owners succeed. If you go to www.whatismanager.com, you can sign up for this series as a free gift. We also produce a product called "Basic Staff Training." It is a unique product that allows business and practice owners to quickly turn their staff into their team, almost as if with the push of a button. It includes a DVD with 35 three minute videos and a workbook. The cost of this series is $2500.00.

Recently, we had a client who owned a chiropractic clinic. We determined that she would benefit greatly from these two products, so while we spoke in my office, I signed her up for the free "Winning Business Tips" series. Each day, for the next several weeks, she would automatically get a three minute video sent to her email regarding important business-building tips. I then talked to her about the other product and sold it to her. It comes in a beautiful package, and she carried the package proudly out of the office.

Usually within a week of our clients starting the series, we get a phone call in which they tell us how much they are enjoying the information. This doctor, however, was silent. Another week went by, and so I decided to call to see how she and her staff were doing with the two different products. She was confused.

"I don't have two different products. I just have the videos that I get in my email each day."

Now I was confused. "Doc," I said, "remember when you walked out of the office with our box that says 'Basic Staff Training' on it? Remember how I even showed you the commercial we made, the one that said 'think inside the box?'"

She said that she thought that this was the same video series she was receiving via email. I once again clearly explained the difference between the two products, and asked her if she could please start watching the "Basic Staff Training" videos and start doing the corresponding workbook. I also explained the importance of having her staff start training as well.

Three weeks later, she again had gone silent. I called her office, and she came to the phone. She had not started the staff on the series because she was in the process of hiring someone new. When I asked her if she had started watching it herself, she explained that she thought it was just for her staff to watch. Wow. What the hell do you say to this?

Once again, I explained that as an executive of her own practice, she needed to have this information. Regardless of whether or not her staff ever went through it, she needed to start. Finally, a light turned on, and she got it.

"Oh," she exclaimed, "you think I should do this as well?"

"Yes, please!"

She finally started after only one more phone call, and only after three months of nudging. As a consultant, it is hard to express the level of frustration this type of behavior causes. This was, indeed, an inconvenience for me, but there's more to it than that. It's downright unsafe for us to have "zombified" individuals around driving cars, operating machinery and producing products. It puts all of us at risk.

People who make good hypnotic subjects are not thinking; they are simply reacting. You speak to them, and it goes in one ear and out the other. You ask them to retain some small amount of information, and, several days later, they don't even remember speaking to you. You ask staff members to follow a basic business pattern, and their lack of ability to retain information makes them unemployable. They are then thrown into unemployment, and their burden to society becomes even larger.

If you have recognized, in my writing, some semblance of truth, then hopefully it explains your own personal observations regarding the actions and reactions of those around you. Take solace in the fact that you are not out there, walking through the vast wasteland of the overly-medicated, alone. I hope that it's clear from these observations that the hope for our future lies not in another prescription, but in the awakening of the individual spirit.

Accepting Without Questioning

"Judge a man by his questions rather than by his answers."
-Voltaire

* * *

Recently my fifteen-year-old nephew, Michael, called to ask me if he could spend the day at my podiatry office. He was contemplating future careers and was including medicine as a possibility. I happily agreed, and we made arrangements for him sleep over my house so that we could get started bright and early. On our ride in, I questioned him about what he wanted to get out of the visit. In short, he wanted a better perspective on what was entailed in being a doctor and running a practice.

Well if that was what he wanted, that was what I was going to deliver. In fact, he probably got more than he bargained for. Throughout the day, I kept the poor kid running between patients, all while downloading my philosophy of practice management and life upon him.

For me it was exhilarating. I really enjoyed the opportunity of spending the quality time. But I have to say I wasn't sure if he felt the same. It was hard to judge if he was paying attention or if he was bored. Like most teenagers he spent half of the time listening and half the time texting. In fact, by the time I dropped him off at my sisters, I was unsure if I had delivered the information he was seeking. Perhaps I could put that better; I was sure I had delivered the information, I just wasn't sure that he had paid attention to it.

I felt some consolation when my sister called me later that evening to tell me how thrilled Michael was with the experience. I actually took a sigh of relief and went on my merry way.

What happened next was one of the most beautiful and shocking moments of my life. At 8pm I received a text from Michael that if written on paper would have easily filled several pages. It was labeled "Uncle Dan's Rules for Success," and included almost every word I had spoken throughout the day. Every anecdote, every concept, everything! Not only had he been paying attention, he had absorbed far more than I imagined. It was amazing, he was like a giant sponge, he included things I didn't even remember saying.

It is hard to express in words the impact his gesture had on me. Suffice it is to say it concluded a verbal contract we had with each other. I guess we both delivered and received more than we each had expected. His text was worth more to me than all the gold in "Fort Knox" (if there still is any?).

This is an example of a verbal contract honored by both sides. Although not written, it was implied by the fact that he was spending the day in my office, that I would give him a worthwhile experience. In exchange I would receive some indication that the information was of value and was appreciated. It was a win-win situation, both of us walking away feeling to some degree changed for the better.

It certainly would be nice if agreements could be so easily implied and held to in the business arena. However due to the complex and often muddied nature of these associations, a written contract is needed. In a perfect world, these written contracts would clarify the forward actions and rewards of both parties. Unfortunately, this is often not the case. In fact, many times the contracts presented to us are designed to mislead, to focus attention on one clause, while pulling a "rabbit out of the hat," regarding another.

Remember that words can trap you as much as they can free you. Others can change the meaning of words, and before you know what you have agreed to, the beast can be upon you!

The experience of a family friend will bring this point home nicely. This individual owned and ran two rather large medical imaging facilities. Because of his advancing age, he decided it was time to slowdown, to take time to "smell the roses." His solution was to put one of the facilities up for sale. He placed ads in the appropriate medical journals and immediately received a qualified response. His legal team sprung into action, carefully drafting a sales contract. This was presented to the potential buyer, who, likewise, drew upon the skills of his attorneys. Some modifications were made and the ball was placed back in the "court" of my friend.

Not wanting to incur any further legal fees, he briefly glimpsed over the changes, and unfortunately put his signature on the dotted line. Unbeknownst to him, and as unbelievable as it may seem, the buyer's attorney had included the purchase of both facilities in the sale agreement. Since both facilities were incorporated under the same name, adding the second address was an almost innocuous yet dramatic change. The purchaser got a "two for one deal," and my friend got an additional year of legal fees, and the lesson of his life. Whether this was an honest miscommunication or a deliberate plundering is speculation, it's devastating effects were not.

This example points out how after making a verbal agreement or written contract, the outcome can still be completely the opposite of that which was anticipated. Yet, contracts still remain the binding words of our society. In business, be sure to sign on the dotted line only when you understand every word in the contract, and the context in which the words are utilized. Protect your future by assuring that what you have signed your name to is, in fact, what you have agreed upon.

On the school playground, bullies rely on their size and their contacts. If they are bigger than you or can surround you with others who are, you become the target. As these individuals have grown older, as they have fought their way up the corporate ladder or found themselves in leadership positions, the one thing that has often not changed are their personalities. A bully is often in fact, a coward, lacking in knowledge and deficient in capacity. But they can be persistent, they can be intelligent and they certainly can be drawn to positions of power. They fear those who have better ideas and have the ability to swiftly put those ideas into action. Similarly, they fear those who can respond with quick and targeted actions. That fear can drive them harder, push them farther then one might imagine. They live in a world in which they are constantly at risk for being exposed. Therefore they envision the "perfect world" as one in which others can be kept under their thumb. Much like cockroaches exposed to a bright light, they scurry for cover under the direct scrutiny of those with wisdom and courage. They inherently fear what I spoke of previously: knowledge and chutzpah.

In response to these weapons, they have developed a highly effective defense mechanism. It is one that deflects the light of truth away from their dark caverns, and into the vast expanses of space. They hide behind words. They wrap their victims in paperwork. They tighten their strangle from a distance. They give no immediate target for reprisal. And, finally, they have brilliantly evolved bureaucracies. I said they were bullies, but I did not say they were stupid.

Positions that allow for the establishment and expansion of these defense mechanisms can often be magnets for this personality type. Although, this is not to say that every politician is a bully, it is to say that political positions in general can often be quite alluring to him or her. It is also to say that, with what we know about decent, altruistic individuals, given the tincture of time, and no warning mechanism, any political system would ultimately be overrun by those who would, at the very least, be self-serving, and, at the very worst, be destructive of freedom.

If you think that there's someone out there who would never let bad things happen, and that surely some automated system will protect you, other than point you in the direction of history, I would like to share with you one lesson from my past experiences.

As a generalization, decent, ethical people tend to be quieter than evil people. Decency shows itself in those who are content, sitting back, watching the grandchildren eat and play. Decency does not, for the most part, obsess over attention and power. More often than not, it wants to be left alone. Decency cannot imagine evil, and, when facing it, will rationalize it in the direction of good. Evil, on the other hand, is aggressive, obsessed and driven. Evil can only survive in conquest, as it does not create, but, rather, it feeds. Couple these two basic concepts, and we see the parable of the sheep and the wolf. Often, the sheep does not see the wolf until it's too late.

Fortunately, though, we are not sheep, and we can be made more alert. We can develop warning systems, like bells and whistles that go off as the pack stealthily approaches. In the 1980's movie "The Fog" by John Carpenter, a killer fog torments a northern California fishing town. The actress Adrienne Barbeau plays a radio disc jockey stationed in a lighthouse overlooking the town. Her broadcasts of the whereabouts of the incoming fog help rescue countless numbers of townspeople. Ultimately, the fog retreats, and the town survives.

Our movie can be entitled "The Bureaucracy." It can tell the tale of a relentless and creeping bureaucracy slipping into the country and threatening to obliterate all of its freedoms. It slips under the door jams, and it advances through the televisions, radios and computer screens. It surrounds us with certifications and overbearing insurance requirements, and it makes every motion potentially illegal, or at least suspicious. It is THE BUREAUCRACY!

Bullies among us, drawn to the most powerful positions, have developed an almost perfect defense mechanism. Still, fortunately for us, it is not perfect, because now you know. As a defense mechanism, it is only powerful when utilized on an unsuspecting populace. An informed citizenry simply pushes it aside to see the small, shriveled individuals pulling the oversized levers. Jokingly, one may find it reminiscent of "The Wizard of Oz," yet we know in our hearts that it's more threatening than a standing army.

Mark this notion down in bold letters, and remember these words always. Compare the physical number of bureaucratic requirements from year to year, even if those requirements sound good, and even if they dictate that we all must get chocolate ice cream every Sunday or a free lunch every Monday. The following applies strictly to the number, and pays no attention to the content:

The greater the increase in bureaucratic requirements in society, the larger the number of bullies holding positions of power in that society!

Keep Your Eyes on the Prize

"You can become blind by seeing each day as a similar one. Each day is a different one, each day brings a miracle of its own. It's just a matter of paying attention to the miracle."
-Paulo Coelho, One of Brazil's most successful novelists.

* * *

The majority of this book, up to this point, has been of a defensive nature. It has been about pointing out potentially difficult obstacles, raising your awareness of them and offering what I have found to be some workable solutions. Now, I would like to gently take you into the direction of some more offensive strategies. But, before I do, I would like to point out that only concentrating on the obstacles, only being aware of the negativity in people and only living a life of caution is not living. It is also not the point of this book. Dangerous people and conditions do exist, and being aware of that is important. But becoming *only* aware of the negative aspect of that reality completely misses the boat.

In life, as in business, there are times when we can become jaded. We can begin to lose faith in our fellow man. And, yet, if we look closely, there are acts of heroism and selflessness being done around us all the time. The problem is that when they are done, there are no fireworks marking them from above. There's no news reporter jumping out from behind the trees to report on that extra smile or that pat on the back. Still, these small acts of decency have profound effects on those who are privileged enough to witness them.

Such is the case I witnessed in my second year of podiatry school. My roommate and best friend was Stephen Markantone. Steve and I were Frick and Frack. We did everything together, from hitting the pubs to hitting the books.

On one particular day, we were deep in the throes of finals. We had gone to class in the morning, studied some in the afternoon, and then walked the mile and a half distance to the gym to pump some iron. We cut our workout short on this particular evening, because our next day's test was on neuroanatomy, and the test was simply impossible.

Both Steve and I figured that we would be studying from 8pm that evening until 1am in the morning, and that therefore we should be okay to pass. When we got back to our dorm apartment, another student (nicknamed "Alabama" because of his home state) was waiting. He needed help with another class, and he was upset because he was potentially failing out. This schmuck had all week to come by, but he chose the night before this major final to ask for tutoring on a completely different subject. I looked at him, and was about to mouth the words "good luck" when Steve invited him in.

I excused myself, went into my room and began to study. One hour later I came out, and there were Steve and Alabama deep into a full-blown tutoring session.

I pulled Steve to the side and asked him what he was doing. "How the hell are you going to study yourself if you spend all night tutoring him?"

Steve answered, "I feel bad. I can't let him fail out."

Believe it or not, Steve stayed up for most of the night tutoring Alabama, and then spent the rest of the night catching himself up. I, on the other hand, was tucked into bed by 1am.

When I woke up in the morning, poor Steve looked like he had been run over by a tractor trailer. Somehow, he still managed to pull off a high grade on this final. Either way, this was really a selfless act, and to this day it is something I often reflect on when I think of people who have demonstrated greatness. It was profoundly kind.

Although Alabama passed his test, can you believe that he never thanked Steve? He never, in any way, acknowledged what was done for him. If I could light off fireworks to thank Steve on behalf of Alabama, I would. My words in this book will, however, have to suffice.

By merely observing selflessness, the effect that it had on me has raised my own abilities to a different level. I understand friendship far better because of watching someone else demonstrate it. We become jaded because there are spotlights on horrific acts, and yet the decent acts are left in the shadows. I, for one, am all for turning the lights up on those who truly deserve them. When you do, you will see that goodness surrounds you.

I have another example of this concept, and while it may seem small to you, that's sort of the point. It's the small, everyday good acts that should have our attention. This is where life can be at its most beautiful.

Several months ago I was driving with my daughter. She was strapped into her child seat, and we were singing songs and having a wonderful time. Suddenly, she interrupted with a question that almost had me veer the car off of the road.

She asked, "Daddy, what is a debate?" I looked in the rear view mirror in disbelief. That is one heck of a question for a five year old, I thought.

I explained that a debate is when one person has one viewpoint and another has a different viewpoint, and that they then try to convince each other of the correctness of their own view. She responded with, "Oh, I had a debate."

I asked who her debate was with, and what it was about. She explained that another girl in her class had said that there was no such thing as God, and my daughter argued that there was a God.

Then, she said, the teacher walked over. Now my daughter really had my attention. When I asked my daughter what the teacher said, my daughter informed me that the teacher told them that there was a God. I smiled, and said, "Well, Alexis, it looks like you won the debate." What she said next could best be summed up with the word "enlightening."

"I won the debate, and God won the debate," she beamed. I held tight to the steering wheel to prevent us from sliding off into the embankment. Here was a five year old child taking on the responsibility of defending God. A small act, done for the right reasons, can have a greater impact than a large act done for the wrong reasons.

Survival of the Fittest

"Give me six hours to chop down a tree and I will spend the first four sharpening the axe."
-Abraham Lincoln

* * *

The best guarantor of future success is planning in the present. You would never think of driving home if you did not have your home address memorized, and if you could not approximate the length of time it would take to reach your destination. Life and business are no different. If you do not have an outline, a map and a game plan, your strategy depends on luck. Since luck does not exist without planning, that really is no plan at all.

Planning for success can be similar to planning for a hierarchy of needs. We would plan for that which was most important first, then that which was slightly less important and so on, until we had accomplished our goal. It turns out that one can compare surviving in the wilderness to surviving in the business world, using very simple analogies:

Hierarchy of needs in wilderness survival:
1) Shelter
2) Water
3) Food

Hierarchy of needs in business survival:
1) Personal ability
2) Money
3) Expansion

If you were dropped into the jungle with only a pocket knife, you would only survive if you understood the hierarchy of actions needed. In a survival situation, your first course of action would be to secure a shelter. This would include, if given enough time, the warmth and protection of a fire. Next would be to secure a source of drinkable water. Third would be to secure food. The reasoning is quite simple: without shelter and fire, given a cold enough environment, you could die of hypothermia within hours. Hypothermia occurs when your body temperature suddenly cools to below 96 degrees F, or 35.5 degrees C.

Without water, you would only last three to four days. Without food, you could last several weeks. As you can see, that which created the greatest threat would be confronted first. The same concept applies to surviving in the business world. Without personal ability, you will never make it out of the gate. Without money, you will not be able to stay in the game, and without expansion, the game will eventually fade away. Let's break this down in more detail.

First, like a shelter, you will need to find a stable area from which you could be secure and protected. Here in business, as in life, you are your own base. You must be at peace with yourself, confident in your abilities and warm in the glow of your own knowledge. Here, I am talking about real knowledge. If you are a plumber, you had better be the best damn plumber you can be. If you are a doctor, you had better be one hell of a clinician, and if you are an artist, your art had better sing. You have to be great at what you do, and what you do had better have some exchangeability.

In other words, being trained in building homes makes sense because you can build a home in which someone could live and better survive. Being trained as a dentist would similarly produce worthwhile products. On the other hand, being trained in sociology or psychology is pretty much a waste of your resources, at this point. If you want to study something because you are interested in it as a hobby, do that later. Right now, you need to learn and acquire abilities that others find valuable and have proven they will exchange for. Nobody in a difficult economy is going to exchange very much for your sociology or psychology degree. Sorry, but it's just not going to happen. You need to gain confidence and you need to gain abilities, but, just as in a survival setting, certain training would be more beneficial than other training. So, in life, as in the jungle, some knowledge is a waste of time, whereas other knowledge is a saving grace. In a survival scenario, it would be far more important to have familiarity with wild, edible plants than to understand the mating habits of the salamander. All knowledge is not equal!

Whatever you have to do to get to that point of confidence, do it. If you have to learn a new skill, then learn it. You have to fix your attention on the future, and on creating that future. If your attention is on a past upset with someone, then handle that upset, but handle it so that you never again devote attention to it, and so that you may move forward without baggage. Do it quickly, as this should not be a lifelong project. Make up any damage you feel you have done to others, and put your attention on building a better future. If the person or persons will not let you make it up, then move on without them.

Make a decision to not make the same mistakes again, and accept that as the best you can do. There is no abundance of time for you to figure out how to survive better, and how to help those around you survive better. Putting any more attention on the past is a luxury that this generation no longer has. Past generations have used up our resources and time. They have left us, for the most part, on our own. The fact that they have failed to recognize this and warn us does not change our predicament. We are, as a culture, in deep doody. Therefore, you have a responsibility, for your progeny and future generations, to be successful and to help pull us out of this. Many hands make light work, and, well, right now we need all the hands on deck that we can find.

The best way I know of to gain personal ability and to build your personal shelter is to jump right in and learn on the fly. Gain confidence as you gain victories. Just don't make any major blunders. Don't sell the house to invest in an untested franchise. Learn on a gradient, and start right from where you are, but start! Learn what you need to learn, point yourself in the direction you desire, and then take that first step. Being secure and confident in your abilities affords one the opportunity to generate power. It is this power that will propel you forward into the next challenge.

Now that you have built your personal shelter, and now that you feel comfortable in your abilities, you are finally able to produce worthwhile and exchangeable products. After finding shelter in a survival scenario, you would acquire water. This is analogous in the business arena to the acquisition of money or exchange. Money is a flow and it is a current, and even the terminology surrounding it is the same terminology that we use when we speak about water. Currency comes from currents. Just as the sides of rivers are called banks, money is held and directed by banks. In fact, most of the laws that govern our courts are no longer based on "laws of the land," but, rather, "laws of the sea," also called Uniform Commercial Codes (UCC). Laws of the sea might also be considered laws of money. Its endpoint is not justice, but the acquisition of finance. Money rules this system, and if you have enough of it, you can pretty much buy your way out of almost any situation. If you have too little of it, tag—you're it!

Remember, however, that money is not an endpoint, as water is not a solid, but a flow. Money comes in, and money goes out. You want to set up this flow so that it runs as consistently and as closely to your shelter as possible. In other words, you want to figure out a system that creates as much consistent money, but with as little effort as possible. Usually, in this stage, it is accomplished by figuring out what you can sell and how to sell it. If you don't know how to sell, you'd better confront that problem, and if you simply don't have anything to sell, go back to step one.

The point here is that most people underestimate how much of a flow they require, and how consistent it actually needs to be so that they may survive. Since this is often the hardest area to confront, it is often done as a last minute action, out of urgency. We need money to pay the rent, so we sell something. Oh no, payroll is due, start making some phone calls. Using environmental pressures to determine how much attention is really given to closing the deal is a lazy point of view. Closing the deal and selling far beyond the level of bare necessity is imperative.

There is a saying in survival situations that "one is none." In other words, if you have only one radio, you really have none because there is a risk that it will break or malfunction. If you are just depending on that one radio for information, you have set yourself up for disappointment. We can see that a far safer goal would be to have at least two radios, because if one breaks, at least we have a backup. An even better preventative solution might be to acquire three radios. There is safety in abundance.

When speaking of money or barter in this economy, "one is none" is the understatement of the year. If you have only enough money to buy one car, one home and one pair of shoes, you are violating this basic principle. Shockingly, in the financial arena, this rule "one is none" should probably be changed to "ten is one" or "twenty is two." I believe that this type of phrase would demonstrate a more realistic level of financial necessity to shoot for, as far as your survival is concerned.

Stop thinking small! You've got to make your financial goals much greater than you've been led to believe you should. In fact, you must make all of your goals much greater than you've been led to believe. No governmental agency is going to save you from the inevitable financial devastation that is coming down the pike. You are it, and the buck stops with you. You have to make all of your goals, whether financial, personal, charitable, relationship-wise or familial far, far greater. You have to get excited again about everything! The opportunities exist all around you, but you have to decide that you will seek them out and take advantage of them. You have to believe in yourself more than you believe in anyone else. You have to learn as much as you can, so that you can handle the first two survival areas I have outlined.

In this "water" stage, you have to put your attention on closing every deal that comes your way. You might have to burn the midnight oil while trying to figure out exactly how to accomplish that. You see, it is crucial that you figure out just what, exactly, you have to say and how to say it, in order to get that signature on the dotted line. Do everything you can to get your product or service delivered, and to get that cash in your hand.

People observing you at this stage should feel tired just watching you work at your intense level of action. They should marvel at how much you accomplish in one day. They should be asking you questions about which vitamins you take and how much money you make. Now, action does not necessarily mean doing. Action can be overseeing. No matter which actions you take in this stage, you will have to do some seriously hard work.

Have you got something better to do with your time? I assure you that if you get your speed up, raise your level of urgency and totally commit to being successful, that somehow, someway, you will be able to fit all the other important parts of your life into your schedule. Once you have a massive flow of funds heading in your direction, direct it, channel it and then go get some food.

Now we reach the third stage of survival. You have acquired the appropriate knowledge, you are producing great products or services, and you are selling those products or services at a reasonable level. At last, your basic needs are met, but that's what they are: basic needs. In this stage, we begin to look for food. In the jungle, we might be gathering edible plants, or dropping a trout line or setting up a rabbit trap. In business, we are now looking to feed our dreams. We are looking toward expansion, and this is where we get our biggest payoff. At this crucial point, we realize that if we don't start to feed our dreams, we start to feed our boredom. This is where the fun stuff happens. This is where we begin to work on not just surviving, but on dominating our field.

You are not concentrating on crushing your competition, because you simply aren't even paying attention to them. You are working toward making them obsolete. You have already established your foothold, your shelter is strong and you have plenty of water. Now you begin to dominate your field at a level that assumes you have no competitors.

Here is where you start to come out of the wilderness. Here is where you let the world know that you did not wait for them to come and rescue you. Here is where you impress them with the fortress that you have built in the middle of the forest. Very soon, you will convince them that this fortress will become a town, and that this town will become a city. Build it, and they will come! Don't forget, though, that you have to be reaching far and wide at this stage. You have to be grabbing attention from as close as possible, and as far away as possible. Let that jungle rattle with the sound of your roar. You have to be screaming, "Look at me, look at what I have accomplished and look at what you too can accomplish with my help!"

Push your communication to the masses, and produce incredible products, all the while screaming. Help massive numbers of people, and yet continue pushing. Success is in the abundance, and just to clarify once again: I am not simply talking about money and finance. I am saying that here, in this arena, is where all of your dreams can feast.

There are those of you who are uncomfortable by the thought of taking this much action, and, therefore, receiving this much attention. Some of you are afraid of the amount of communication in which you will have to take part. The question is: does it make you more uncomfortable than living an "average" lifestyle? Keep in mind that the "average" lifestyle is dying very, very quickly. Only you can answer that question, and, quite frankly, I am not beating the drum for the TV dinner lifestyle.

Only about 20% of people will take what I, and many others, are saying, and run with it. The average "Joe" will not buy into the concept of setting massive goals and putting them into action. Most can't even remember the goals they had set last New Year's Eve. The concept of "one is none" may be wasted on those who don't even have one goal.

Hopefully that is not you. I hope that you recognize your real potential. You can imagine the impact that a fresh, aggressive attitude would have on you, your friends, your family, your favorite charity, your church, temple or house of worship. The average "Joe" in America is going broke, financially, as well as emotionally. A life in which you have been convinced that you are unworthy of reaching your goals, or that your goals are simply unattainable, is not a life of freedom, but it is the life of a prisoner.

The real food of life is in the accomplishment of one's goals, and of this you are capable. Not only must you believe this, but you must act upon it immediately. Your future starts with this moment, and you must decide to make your life far better and far more effective than anyone has ever asked you to do. I am asking you to help lead the way, in order to help create a future in which we will be proud to let our children play. Certainly, you would agree that setting higher goals would at least give you a margin of safety.

Here is a small exercise to guide you in that direction:

1) Make a list of every excuse you have for not achieving the goals you would like to achieve. Remember: an excuse is simply an obstacle to overcome.
2) Make the decision to overcome them!
3) Now, decide to start overcoming them at this instant!
4) Start!

Confronting the Close

"I knew a man who grabbed a cat by the tail and learned 40 percent more about cats than the man who didn't."
- *Mark Twain*

* * *

One of the reasons that most businesses fail in their first few years is not a lack of viable ideas, or even worthy products. It is being unable to be confrontational when it comes to asking for the sale and closing the deal. It's an inability to ask for the moola, and to have the client sign on the dotted line. You see, it is way easier to confront the creativity of an idea, to paint the walls or tighten up the grammar. Even salespeople seem to have an easier time straightening up the stock in the back room than selling off the stock in the front room.

You need creativity, you need great ideas, and you need to get lost in the dream of future products. However, you only earn the time to do that once you have banked the daily nut and paid the daily overhead. This may seem to be an obvious statement, but once you have a worthwhile product or service to sell, your main job is to sell it, period! There is no point in daydreaming about tomorrow if you can't pay the overhead today. Every action of yours has to revolve around selling every day, and selling as much as possible. Everything else in your life can be squeezed in, in the time thus bought. Please get the point that you are buying time for expansion by closing the deal right here, right now. As a business owner or successful entrepreneur, your main thrust has got to be about increasing your bottom line today, then tomorrow, then next week, and then next year. But, it starts with today. Merely having an idea does not a business make. Selling the idea, the product or the service is being in business. It is in the action of closing the deal that the business becomes viable.

Who is a potential buyer for your product? Make a list of everyone you could close a deal with right now. Start calling and closing them! Make them an offer they can't refuse. Get creative, but close the deal. Set a financial target, and don't stop calling and closing until it has been met. Keep increasing those targets. Whatever time is left in the day you may use for administrative organization, future planning or daydreaming, for that matter.

As an executive, your main concern rests first and foremost with making sure your organization is financially viable. Always push in the direction that brings in massive amounts of income. It takes a lot of confrontation skills to do that. It takes much more of those skills than it does to dream. However, closing the deal, paying the bills and stashing away reserves keeps the doors open long enough for your dreams to become reality. Many do the opposite: they keep adding to their dreams, perfecting all of the small details, and yet they miss the biggest one of all, which is that it takes massive amounts of finance to survive in this economy.

Once you have earned the income, you should allocate money for marketing, saving, etc. The point is that all of your problems go away if you can close that deal, make enough money and help enough people. Money is, after all is said and done, simply the scorecard that tells you how many people you have helped. It is, therefore, the main statistic that your attention should be focused on.

If earning income means having to get in your car and drive to the client, so be it. If you have to work evenings or weekends, so what? It is much easier to work on creating your dreams than to work on barely surviving. Business is based on one's ability to generate energy. For example, your ability to get yourself fired up to give that lecture or meet that new client requires energy. You need energy to get excited about that new marketing campaign. That energy, if directed appropriately, results in exchange or money. The energy you generate is what you get paid for. This energy starts within yourself, and it is a force that thrusts you forward.

A 10 horsepower engine has far less forward thrust than a 200 horsepower engine. A $100,000 per year business has far less thrust than a $1,000,000 per year business. Your ability to generate energy within yourself, if channeled correctly, has higher horsepower, or force. When your generated force is greater than the environment's force, you win. If you think that the environment is not constantly generating a force against you, try not paying your mortgage for several months. Watch the force generated by the banks as they kick you to the curb.

Now the question is about how much force you need. Is it okay to generate just enough energy to hold the environment at bay? No way! Holding the environment at bay will ultimately leave you bested. You see, the environment is too massive, and it can generate force as a constant stream, forever.

You may not simply match the force applied against you. Let's say you generate just enough money to pay the mortgage and eat three square meals a day. Eventually you will tire. Once you tire, the game is over. The leverage goes to the environment. You need enough forward momentum to break through the critical mass. It is essential that you break through that critical force of "just barely making it." You have to blow through it so violently that it gives way. Once you have the forward momentum, you keep up the pressure and you don't stop. You keep pushing.

This is when it gets easier and easier. Now your momentum can be leveraged further against the environment. Now luck will begin to appear. Now you can hire more people, and you can expand your facility. Still, even at this level, you must always keep your force directed. You must keep it pushing forward. As you add people, recognize that most do not operate using this concept. They can't generate their own energy, and so they are attracted to your energy.

These energy suckers are like neighbors in a blackout, wanting to hook up to your generator. They will suck away enough energy to put out your lights as well. Your goal is to bring people on board who will hook their generators up alongside of yours and add to your output rather than detract from it. Now, this is far easier said than done. Most people in our society have lost the ability to generate energy. They simply search out those neighbors who have the lights on and attempt to plug in. As an executive, your job is to keep your generator constantly running, and constantly generating more and more force. You must prevent others from tapping your flow, and insist that they add to it. The more people you add, the more energy you should be producing, and the more your bottom line should improve. No excuses! If you get people to power their generators next to you and you don't feel the combined abundance of energy, let them read this chapter. If that doesn't snap them into production, it's time to have them unplug.

The successful entrepreneur must obsessively push the demand for income. Close every deal as fast as you can, and remember that it is called the bottom line for a reason.

Be Willing to Reinvent Yourself

"The simple willingness to improvise is more vital, in the long run, than research."
— *Rolf Potts, Vagabonding*

* * *

Years ago, it was pretty much a given that you would start working for a company after college, and as long as you did your job, you could expect a nice retirement package and a life-long commitment from that company. Those days are long gone. Companies start up, go under and are bought up within the blink of an eye.

Just as quickly, employees are hired, fired, downgraded and upgraded. It is a roller coaster of insanity! With each upward and downward gyration, opportunities are born, and opportunities are removed. No one entering the work force is immune to the roller coaster's thrashing. In fact, those who jump on the roller coaster and expect only a smooth ride are often found jumping off the ride at its lowest level.

This roller coaster ride began early in the 1970's and was fully in swing by the 80's. In fact, I remember driving in my car in the late 80's and listening to The Bob Grant Talk Show on the WOR radio station out of New York. An elderly caller was making a point that I have never forgotten. He explained that he was in his late sixties, and that, growing up, the thing to do was start your own business and make your own way. Recently, however, he had to give advice to his grandchild, who was approaching working age.

His advice was to get a government position. His reasoning was based on retirement benefits. It was an interesting conversation, in which he pointed out that, based on the pensions of government employees, police officers, etc., you can work for twenty years and then get your pension. He pointed out that it would almost be financially impossible for a private business owner to put away enough money in twenty years to collect an equivalent pension. The pendulum had swung away from the private business owner, and had favored the government class.

Almost thirty years later, I often think of that caller and how true his words had been. He even insisted that his grandchild stay completely out of the private sector, which included working for private corporations. Private corporations, he explained, would ultimately fold under the pressure of government subsidies, and be unable to accommodate the pension pressures for government employees. The private sector would ultimately collapse, leaving a government class.

Wow—his words were, for the most part, quite accurate. If you think about working in a government position for 20 years, then getting a percentage of that salary for the rest of your life, it sounds pretty hard to resist. It's almost impossible to duplicate this in the private sector. If you were smart enough to take advantage of one of those pensions, then good for you. Unfortunately, for the rest of us, the government cannot give anything without taking it away from someone else. Eventually, the pendulum swings back again. I bet that if I could have a conversation with that caller, who is probably long deceased, he would be stunned by the level of his own accuracy. The pendulum started at the American dream of owning your own business and of making your own way. It then shifted to the idea of working for a large corporation and getting job security. Then it moved on to the idea of becoming a government employee, where, after 20 years, you take the pension and run.

As the pendulum reverses its trajectory, most Americans stand cowering in fear. The pensions that were promised after many decades of work are tenuously invested, at best. The taxes that helped grow the government have expanded to sizes that no one has anticipated, and they threaten to devour even the meager morsels of a lifetime's work that remain. You would be hard-pressed to find someone declaring that these are the best of times. Still, the one great thing about the American spirit is its resilience. Though some will be sliced deeply as the pendulum reverses, a small portion will use its momentum to propel themselves and future generations to greater heights.

This is, after all is said and done, a book for those individuals who understand that times change, and for those who recognize that within that change lies opportunity. This is a book for those who don't put stock in companies or pension plans. This book is *not* for those who put stock in the latest fads or try to keep up with the Joneses, and fall for the countless other middle class traps. This is a book for those who put stock in themselves, and for those who strive to be better than they once were. It's for those who realize that their only competition is the person who they used to be.

This small group, which is probably no greater than 20% of the population, will be the saving grace of society. On their shoulders will be the fate of future generations. As demonstrated throughout history, the other 80% will matter little in this time of immense change. They will merely be the spectators, rooting for whichever side appears to be winning. In the end, however, they too will benefit from those who will prove bold enough to build the next step in the ascension of human kind.

I am not, for the record, speaking of those who believe themselves to be the next illuminated class. Here I am referring to those who feel that they have been illuminated by the fire that Prometheus has stolen from the heavens. These falsely illuminated people will be relegated to the role of a fly in the ointment. Intelligence and true understanding will ultimately place them as no more than paragraphs in the history book of mankind.

This will be a time of the strong, who will not only survive, but thrive. It will be a time when the lessons of thousands of years of mankind will finally be utilized, to give even those who are weaker the opportunity to gain higher footholds until even they became more than they ever believed they could be. As pendulums are prone to swing backwards, this one will come back to the independence and value of the individual. This empowerment will be less dependent on might, and more dependent on intellect. Those who will be sought out will not be those who could more readily throw a ball through a hoop or into the end zone. Those who will be sought out will be those who can best improve the overall conditions of society. The true value of man will be laid out for everyone with honest ambition to follow.

But this is a view of tomorrow, and its outcome is still dependent on the actions of today. Tomorrow's bridges cannot be built without today's ladders. Much like an architect would pull out his blueprints and the tools of his trade, I have laid out some directions, some pit-stops to avoid and some obstacles to circumvent.

Unfortunately, most of the obstacles and pit-stops come in the forms of other people, rather than objects. By clearly identifying several of the more difficult personality patterns, we can draw away our attention from past and present interpersonal entwinements, and look to future visions.

Despite what you have been told, despite the harping criticisms you have heard and despite the horrible economic plight awaiting us, I believe the future to be so bright that you will have to wear shades. Unfortunately, this brightness will only be evident for a small percentage in the beginning. It will be up to these individuals to lead the way for those left behind. Luckily, these future leaders will be born of a different cloth from the leaders of years gone by. They will understand and value the connectedness that binds us all. They will not forget their brethren. They will rise to greater heights, yet turn back, hands stretched for all to grasp. It is at that time that the true greatness, inherent in all of us, will be allowed to shine. The gold-paved streets that beckoned past generations will become more than just a dream.

I am certain of this reality. Notice how the uncovering of hidden history has now becoming a mainstream activity. The reality of this future is evident in the rising tide of skepticism aimed at what is now becoming known as the "dinosaur media." Ask anyone on the street if they trust any of the mainstream news channels, and their laughter will be telling. There is a new thirst for learning the truth and an emerging distaste for what is simply entertainment. This is a thirst that will only be quenched after those who have maintained the status quo have been gently pushed to the side. The dam has begun to break, and there is no way for the status quo to rebuild it. Although we may be way downstream, we can still feel the vibrations of the stones dislodging from their hoisted positions. Those of us who have climbed to higher ground will survive the coming flood.

You now have a choice: Do you sit back and wait to see what happens? Do you hope it will all work out, or do you become inspired? Do you decide right here and right now that you have had enough? Do you decide that your responsibility is to become greater then you have ever imagined, and that you need to increase the volume of your goals? If you were planning on doubling your business this year, times that by ten. If you were planning on multiplying your business by ten, multiply it by twenty. To put it plainly, now is the time to be everything that you ever wanted to be.

This entire book has been written to give you some tools to accomplish just that, but the greatest tool is raising your level of necessity. There is no abundance of time to wait for things to fall into place. You don't have twenty years to build a nest egg and buy that condo in Miami in which you can retire. You are not living in the same world as your grandparents, or even your parents. You have greater opportunities, but on the flip side, you have much, much greater liabilities. Only a few will overcome these liabilities, while the rest will look up to those who overcame as the purveyors of the future.

Which side of the coin will you be on? You do have a choice. In the film "The Matrix," Morpheus gave Neo a choice: you can pick the blue pill and go back to sleep, or you can pick the red pill and face reality. It takes real courage to take the red pill. However, it takes true stupidity to take the blue one. By taking it, you do not go back to sleep just to benefit yourself, but you go back to sleep on all those who depend on you.

Safety for all the ones you love lies in abundance. You need an abundance of love, an abundance of money and an abundance of resources. Abundance! The notion that we can just get by is a trap, and it is a trap that whittles you down to obscurity. We always hear that we should be happy that we have three square meals a day, as some people don't have any food. We are told to be grateful that we just have a job, because some people would die for our position. We are told to be happy that we have a roof over our head and so on.

I am happy when I am producing, I am happy when I am successful and I am happy when I see the positive impact my actions have on those around me. I do not want to be part of the middle class, because the middle class is dying. The middle class is not long for this world. Therefore, to shoot for the middle class lifestyle as a goal would be a fool's error. There is no safety in the middle class. There is no room for error. If you are just making enough money for three squares a day, and suddenly you get injured, what are you supposed to do? Should you settle for two square meals? And are you supposed to be happy, then, because somewhere someone is settling for only one square meal? Is your happiness, therefore, based on the fact that you're not as miserable as someone else? What kind of a dream is that?

"I cried because I had no shoes until I saw someone who had no feet." Wow—that makes me feel better! That poor guy has no feet, and my toes are twinkling away. Cut me a break. I think we can do better than this. Given the right point of view, we are made aware of our true potential, and the stars await. If we have no feet, given our true potential, someone will build us robotic ones. We are not limited, but, rather, we are told that we are limited.

Can you imagine if you grew up in a society where everyone had full faith in your ability to accomplish anything you desired? Can you imagine if the only obstacle was the limit of your imagination? Where would you be right now? This very second, where would you be? If you told me that you would be no further along than you are now, I would be quite surprised.

What if you were raised in an environment where you were told, and were completely convinced, that you had magical powers? What if you were told that anything you ever imagined could come true? What if that entire society were built on a conspiracy to convince you of that fact? Imagine if every teacher you had in elementary school pounded your magical abilities into your head. Imagine if every classmate marveled at your inner power. Imagine if every boyfriend or girlfriend supported you in your pursuit of whatever it was you felt was important to pursue.

Now imagine this society, and really imagine it: Every television sitcom is based on the incredible abilities, creativity and success of the characters. Every news program empowers you with information you can actually use to better your survivability. Would you be the same person if you grew up in that society? The answer is a resounding "no." Instead, you would be a force to be reckoned with, as you would be unstoppable. You would become a leader, the likes of which books are written about. And yet, you would not have been different as a person. The only thing that would be different would be the environment's beliefs. You see, in that environment, the agreement would be that you could accomplish anything. In this society? Not so much.

My daughter is almost six years old. She is truly an amazing kid, and I, for one, want to make sure that she is convinced of her magical powers. I would love to send her to a school that agrees upon and embraces her greatness, but that is a fairy tale. By fairy tale, I'm not referring to magical powers. The fairy tale is the idea that the school would revere her greatness. The intentions of the teachers in that school may be excellent, but they are more concerned that she sits still, whispers during lunch, doesn't run during recess and never talks to strangers.

Have you ever met someone who sits still, speaks so low that you think they are whispering, never runs anywhere and never speaks to strangers? They are your typical middle class worker bee. They never get excited, and they are happy when they are able to make the monthly mortgage payments. They would never think of rocking the boat.

Did you know that if you ever want to get any money, the only people who have it are strangers? If you don't learn to communicate to strangers, who are you going to get that moola from in years to come? This is not a conspiracy to uplift one's potential. In fact, it is the opposite. To the ruling class, a worker bee is more valuable than a killer bee. To the ruling class, a quiet and obedient citizen is more valuable than a wild-eyed poet. But to everyone else, the wild-eyed poet is, if nothing else, a hell of a lot more fun.

In fact, I think we need more poets, more artists and more beauty. I want streets paved with gold. I'm tired of massive New York City pot holes! I declare this moment to be the moment that I raise every expectation and every goal I have to that which would take most people several lifetimes to accomplish. I raise my sights to the accomplishments of the 'Thomas Jefferson's, the 'da Vinci's, the 'Einstein's, the 'George Washington's and the 'Rosa Park's. These are people who stood up when others sat down. These are the ones who embraced and ultimately conquered their fears, catapulting themselves into the very edges of the human experience.

I hereby officially offer up the crutch of my personal losses. I lay aside my baggage, as it is too heavy to carry in the pursuit of my greater goals. I want no stops. Burn the ships, and make the only option that of forward progress. This book is a book of future success. It's of promises we make to ourselves and to each other, to build a better world and to find a better way. If that means working harder, loving stronger, planning better and running faster, so be it! I, for one, have never been afraid of hard work.

There's nothing I have ever accomplished that has come easily. Anything I was ever proud to place my name on pushed the limits of my abilities, and forced me into areas I had never ventured upon before. Never, as I pushed those boundaries, did I feel comfortable. Never, as I pushed, was I not scared. However, I would rather push the boundaries with my intentions. I would rather be scared on my own volition, than be scared on the terms given to me by the environment. As they say, the harder you work, the luckier you get.

There is no greater challenge than the one that lays before you. It does not matter what your goal is, I assure you. You are about to be challenged at a level you might not have seen coming. The incredible level of debt our politicians have inadvertently, or not so inadvertently, signed us onto is appalling. The relentless printing of money by the privately-owned Federal Reserve will result in an inflationary depression, way more profound than what our grandparents lived through.

You may ask me why, in a book about empowerment, after explaining the ultimately positive outlook for the future, would I drop this bombshell upon its reader. There is a saying that forewarned is forearmed. If you know the future, you can prepare for it. You can strengthen your weak points and you can correctly estimate the effort it will take to reach your goals, no matter the storm.

If you are unaware of your opponent, you can easily come up flatfooted and unable to land the knockout punch. This opponent is formidable, and this opponent is three times bigger than you had ever imagined. That is why you have to be ten times bigger than you ever thought you had to be. You see, in order to win this fight, you just have to be that damn big! Your goals have to be huge, and you cannot rest on your laurels. If you do, you will lose, and your loss will be a loss felt by all who surround you. Your loss will be a crushing blow to those who depend upon you.

The environment today is as savage as it ever was. The velvet glove on the iron fist may make it seem less so, but if you are the main breadwinner in your family, try getting sick. Watch how well that works out for your dependents. Our society is smokescreen upon smokescreen. Blowing the smoke is a pride of lions creeping stealthily upon their unwitting prey.

So yes—I am, at this moment, trying to scare the bejesus out of you. This is not because it makes for more entertaining reading, but because it is the truth. They say that in the land of the blind, the one-eyed man is king. If what I am saying here is shocking or unrealistic to you, it is only because you have been walking amongst the blind for so long that your eyesight has diminished. Look around, and really look around. Do you notice that the price of everything is heading upward? Do you see that there are more and more empty storefronts? Do you hear the tales of woe from friends and family? Now, do you really think that my assessment is that far off?

So, what's next? How do we get back from fearful to fearless? My friend, again it comes back to necessity level. Once you realize for yourself how far off from your goals you actually are, you will do one of two things: You will collapse and surrender, which is by far the harder and more dangerous direction. Or, you will take the bull by its horns, and when you come up to bat, you will hit the ball out of the ballpark. I truly hope that you pick the latter, and I hope that the ball flies harder and further than anyone has ever hit it before. Sincerely, this is my wish for you.

The real world requires real action. Hitting the ball out of the park takes massive practice. It may look easy, but it's only easy after you've done it a thousand times. The amount of practice you require also depends on the skill of the pitcher you are going up against. Misestimate the skill of the pitcher, and you misestimate the amount of practice required. L. Ron Hubbard best describes necessity level as: "It is a sudden heightened willingness which untaps a tremendous amount of ability."

Let's look at this concept of necessity level, using a rather silly example: Let's say you were a shoe salesman and I was a mafia kingpin. Now, let's say that you owed me $10,000. You have no money, and you have borrowed as much money as possible from friends and family. I call you and inform you that I need the money by 7pm this evening or things are going to get broken. What would you do? Well, if running and hiding were off the table, you would have to figure out how to raise $10,000 in a few hours.

This pressure might get you to start coming up with ideas that you would never have thought of without it. This pressure might have you doing things that you never would have done previously. Perhaps you might be calling every person who had visited the store in the last year to offer them a discount on any shoe purchased today. Maybe you would be making sure that every single person who walked into your store purchased an item. You could try standing outside the store, handing out fliers for your one day sale. Your closing ratio would go through the roof.

You would do things that you had never done before, because the pressure for survival had been pointed at your head. Your necessity level had become high enough to create an action that was sufficient enough to accomplish the task at hand. I assure you that you would make the $10,000, probably with thirty seconds to spare.

Let's look at a more practical example: In college, when did you finish that final paper? If you're like most of us, you finished it right before it was due. Necessity is the mother of invention, and the bigger the mother, the greater the invention!

Lessons from the Past

"The average man is a conformist, accepting miseries and disasters with the stoicism of a cow standing in the rain."
- *Colin Wilson, British author of* The Outsider.

* * *

Probably one of the biggest reasons people don't succeed to the level that they would like to is that they have never done it before. Now, that may seem like a ridiculous statement, but if you have never felt the thrill of victory, defeat often seems the only plausible outcome.

Yet, how many stories have you heard about a person who was about to give up on a course of action, then gave it one last try and succeeded? It applies to fitness: Adults who have stayed in shape well into their forties and fifties were almost always either athletic as children, or had parents who were. Usually, they had a parental figure who emphasized, in their earlier years, the importance of taking care of one's body. They had experienced being in shape at an earlier time period and were accustomed to the pain of a good workout. In fact, they viewed it not as pain, but as an indication of a successful routine.

Now, let's look at someone in their forties who has never lifted weights. Put them on a bench press for a few light sets and listen to them complain the next day about how sore they are. This soreness, they believe, indicates a need to discontinue, and they prevent any future progress. They have associated pain with a need to stop, and, therefore, they fail to see that it often really indicates smooth sailing ahead. This kind of pain means that you are pushing at a sufficient level, and that something is pushing back at you, which is a job well done. You have heard the saying, "No pain, no gain!" Anything that was ever worth accomplishing had, at its gateway, some form of discomfort. In fact, the greater the reward, the greater the discomfort while achieving it.

If, when you were younger, you saw the most beautiful girl or guy that you had ever seen, and you wanted to strike up a conversation (or even be so bold as to ask them for a date), it was a pretty scary moment, trying to get up your guts. The more taken you were with them, the greater the palm sweat. Now, take the scenario where you really could not care less whether you were going with them or someone else. See? It's not so scary. The reward is small, and therefore the fear is little. This is the model many, many people follow. No fear, no reward. It's just the status quo.

Many come home after work, turn on the television set and chill. Well, if you really want to see someone chill, look at a dead body. That is really chilling! Life is about being hot-blooded. Life only encounters exciting stages when you embrace your fears and push your boundaries. Sitting in front of a television, watching someone else face their fears, is not living. It is being a fly on the wall of your own life.

However, many people, even after hearing these words, still snicker and pick up the remote. Their past failures are still too real for them to confront. They know that they have tried once, and, therefore, they would rather curl up on the couch and let the world beat its path to their door than face the difficulties associated with trying again.

People use past failures as present crutches. NEWSFLASH: No one is beating a path to your door. In fact, no one cares if you decide to never push the boundaries. Ultimately, people want to survive better, and they are drawn to those who they sense can assist them in their survival or the survival of their friends, families or cultures. They are repelled by people who are a drain on their survival. Anyone not pulling the wagon is sitting in the wagon, and after a while the pullers withdraw their consent. They stop pulling, and there goes the society.

So, it would seem that we are all connected. It would seem that the more we can influence people to be in the game, and to push their boundaries in order to create abundance, the better we all will fare.

Since one of the greatest steps toward forward progress is past experiences, let us reflect on the subject of past failures: I remember being a medical student and doing an externship at St. Michael's Hospital in Newark, New Jersey. We were being given a tour of the operating room, when a general surgeon stepped from behind the doorway. I was taken aback by his appearance, as his arms and much of his neck were covered in tattoos. Today this image is far more common, but in the mid-1980's, this was not so prevalent. He began to tell us about the functions of the operating room, and then he stopped. Obviously, he had seen the shocked looks on the faces of the externs, and I could assume that he had been through this before.

He said, "I know you are all looking at my tattoos. Just to explain: in my younger days, I ran with a bad crowd and spent some time in gangs, etc. One day, I woke up and decided to change the direction of my life. Unfortunately, some decisions cannot be reversed. I regret getting all of these tattoos, but I have not let them define me."

"How have your patients reacted?" someone inquired.

"Just like you guys did," he laughed, "but then, when we got down to business, they could see me for who I am, and when you are good at what you do, people inherently recognize your abilities. It hasn't been a great hindrance. "

The rest of the lesson went off without a hitch, and he was correct: I was more enthralled with his knowledge than with his look. I'd like to say I can remember what he was talking about, but I can't. What I did learn, however, was a lesson in human perseverance. Here was someone who turned his life around 180 degrees. He went from gang banger to general surgeon, and with all he had accomplished, his mistakes were still as clear as the nose on his face.

His story has always inspired me. He could just as easily have felt sorry for himself, and thus gone the way of so many. You could say that he chose the hard way, as he faced the pain. But, in fact, he chose the easier route. He gained the respect of many, and to this day I am still writing about his influence on me.

He could have taken our stares and internalized them. He could have felt bad about his look and quietly shut down. Instead, though, he addressed our concerns head-on. He handled and confronted us so that we could move on to see the man behind the mask. That is boldness, that is greatness and that is a life worth speaking about. That is a lesson that they should teach in school. There are no excuses and no crutches. The hand you are dealt is the hand you are dealt. It means nothing, it never has and it is an illusion. You can accomplish anything, no matter your starting point. I'm certain that you, yourself, can think of people who have done similarly. I can write of at least a dozen more, and yet it is always the same story. It summarizes the same way. Against all odds, someone comes forward and beats adversity. In fact, they don't just beat it, they pummel through it. They chew it up and spit it out.

We all sit back and rightfully admire the gumption and the chutzpah. The only mistake we make is that we do not admire that same gumption in ourselves. It is, however, there, waiting to be fed. It's waiting to rise above all the silly reasons we tell it to stay small, stay glued to the television and reflect on past upsets or past negative experiences.

Now, this may seem a novel concept, but the more attention you put on your past failures, the more they become present failures. The more you use past situations as reasons for future handicaps, the less that future will be. And, since no one will really care if you slowly slip into oblivion, why do it? It's not fun, and it's certainly not exciting.

Quite frankly, if you want to attract sympathy as your main means of attention-getting, that too is a trap. People want to be around people they admire, not those with whom they sympathize. If people wanted to surround themselves with those they sympathize with, sixth place in the race would get the biggest trophy. Statues would be erected to honor the accomplishments of the homeless. No, life does not work like that. Instead, the strong survive, and those who were once weak and become strong survive better. Adversity is your friend. When you have reached bottom and have found your way to the top, your fear has been overcome. You have felt it and you have conquered it, and you will always win from that point on.

You have an inner understanding of who you are. No one can ever take that from you. That is the greatest payment life can offer. This is where you get your self-confidence, as well as the ability and knowledge of past conquests and of battles won.

What a gift starting at the bottom is. It is a gift that, once accepted, allows you to find out what your true capabilities are. It is like getting a 1960 Chevy with a Ferrari engine. It doesn't look great until you test it out on the freeway. Once you make the decision to floor the gas, the real power is revealed. Not one person reading this cannot have everything of which they have ever dreamed. They simply have to overcome their past, come to peace with whatever it is they need to come to peace with, make up whatever damages they may have caused and never look back again. Your past is only your friend when you have overcome it. Your past is never your friend when you are awash in it.

Just to continue beating a dead horse for a second, I will share one more quick story that I think will help make my point; hopefully, it will bring some closure to your past upsets, should you have any:

My uncle Mendel was a tall, redheaded man. As a child, I always remember the twinkle in his eyes and his big, broad smile. You could summarize his life by saying that he made the best of everyday and truly enjoyed every moment.

Several days before he died I went to visit him, and, as we talked, he pointed to a framed poem he had on his wall. He told me that this poem had gotten him through the most difficult points in his life, and so he asked me to read it out loud to him. The poem was called "Desiderata" by Max Ehrmann. Here is a few lines of that poem:

"Take kindly to the counsel of the years, gracefully surrendering the things of youth. Nurture strength of spirit to shield you in sudden misfortune. But do not distress yourself with imaginings. Many fears are born of fatigue and loneliness.

Beyond a wholesome discipline, be gentle with yourself. You are a child of the universe, no less than the trees and the stars; you have a right to be here. And whether or not it is clear to you, no doubt the universe is unfolding as it should."

Perhaps you have heard this poem before, but if you have not, the complete poem is certainly worth the read. It had quite a profound effect on me. Now, believe it or not, Mendel was my grandmother Jean's brother. They had grown up in the same difficult environment, and yet he made life more pleasant for all those who knew him. He brought poetry into my life. She brought anger and destruction. It was the same environment, yet with completely opposite results. Why? Life is simply a point of view.

Serendipity

"Serendipity always rewards the prepared."
—Katori Hall, *American playwright, journalist and actress*

* * *

Whether you believe in serendipity, the providing of the universe or dumb luck, we realize that when we are ready, that which we are ready for often appears. When we have prepared for luck, it arrives. When we have not prepared, luck does not exist. As I sat, looking for the final closing to this book and searching for a way to bring home its points in order to tie up its loose ends, it was handed to me. It was handed to me by a chance meeting, where the odds would make Vegas bookies shake their heads in disbelief.

I was sitting at a coffee shop in New York City. I find that writing on paper helps me think more clearly. I had the rough draft of this book piled high in my folder when I accidentally knocked it onto the floor. A woman sitting next to me bent over to help me pick up several of the sheets. I thanked her for her help and she smiled, then asked me what I was so busily writing. I explained that I was writing a book about setting goals, and about making those goals much greater than one ever felt they needed to before. She smiled and she told me that that was what her grandmother had always told her: "Set goals in this lifetime that you would think could only be accomplished in three lifetimes."

She had my attention. "Your grandmother sounds like an amazing woman. Can you tell me about her?" I asked. Here is her story:

The woman's grandmother, Leah, was born on a farm that was deep in the countryside of Brazil. She was one of twelve children, and they were very poor. When Leah turned seventeen, she decided that this was not the life that she wanted to lead.

She simply got up and walked into the woods, and just kept walking. Two days later, she made it to a small town. When she arrived at the town, she heard a man yelling in the street about the circus opening that evening. She walked up to him and asked what a circus was. From what this woman told me, her grandmother was beautiful, but her haggard appearance and the rags she was wearing took this man by surprise. He asked her why she was dressed so poorly, and so she explained her journey. She also wanted to know more about the circus. This was her first time seeing what we might consider civilization, and one could just imagine her excitement. This gentleman felt so sorry for this country bumpkin that he gave her money to buy food, some nicer clothes and a place to bathe and sleep. He also, as it turns out, was the owner of the circus, and invited her to that evening's debut.

She ate a meal, bought some new clothes and spent her first night in civilization at the circus. She was so taken by the performances that she asked this gentleman if she could work for him. He agreed, and she became the hardest working person he had ever seen. After several years he came to depend on her, and he offered her a small percentage of ownership. She became his limited partner. Several years later, she had saved up enough money and bought a larger share. Ultimately, she bought the entire circus.

What was even more astonishing, however, was that she also bought several hotels and the main gambling casino in one of the local towns. She accomplished all this within twenty years. She even sent for her brothers and sisters, whom she would employ for the rest of their lives.

This young woman had stepped from out of the woods with tattered clothes, yet with immaculate confidence. She knew that she could accomplish whatever she set out to accomplish, no matter the odds. I marvel at the courage that she must have had to simply leave the life she had known. She was stepping into the darkness of the woods, yet, ultimately, into the beginning of her dreams. To hear this woman speak of her grandmother, you could only imagine the power this individual exuded. She spoke of the impact that her grandmother had on her life, and how she had always been told to "dream the dreams of three lifetimes."

She attributed all of her success to this incredible woman. I thanked her for this amazing story and asked if she would mind if I used it in my book. Thankfully, she stated that it would be wonderful to have someone put Leah's story into words. I asked her for her name and what she did. She was a fashion designer for high-end ladies' bathing attire.

I was not up on my fashion designers, so her name did not ring a bell. When I got home that evening and told my wife the story, however, my wife instantly knew who this woman was. The following weekend, while watching television, the news covered her fashion show at Lincoln Center in Manhattan. It turns out that she was one of the top ladies' bathing suit designers in the world. Leah had obviously impacted her granddaughter, and, presumably, all those who came into contact with her.

A young woman stepping into the woods almost one hundred years ago created such an effect that it embodies every story, every ideology and every thought I have tried to convey. Today is the day that you, too, can step into the woods and into your great adventure. Today you can "dream the dreams of three lifetimes," and make them your reality. Your future awaits.

About the Author

Dr. Daniel Margolin is the author of *Fast Tracking Your Prosperity*, offering timeless practical advice for success in business and in life.

Margolin is the owner of the New Jersey Foot & Ankle Center in Oradell, New Jersey. Board certified in podiatric surgery, podiatric orthopedics, and primary podiatric medicine, he has been in practice since 1987 and has treated well over 25,000 patients.

Margolin is also the founder and co-owner of Effective Management, a consulting company specializing in business expansion strategies. He and his business partner, Justin Feinberg, are the inventors of video-assisted technology amplification, which can be used to create an array of business training tools, including basic staff training, professional public relations and marketing, successful sales, and beginning business strategies. They are continually developing new and improved methods for delivering business organizational, management, and marketing techniques.

He currently resides with his wife and daughter in New Jersey. For further information contact him at dan@effectivemanagement.net

22457485R00095

Made in the USA
Middletown, DE
31 July 2015